Growing Up a Chatham Islander
On the Edge of 44 Degrees South

Growing Up a Chatham Islander

On the Edge of 44 Degrees South

by
Val Mete

Copyright © Val Mete, 2012. All rights reserved.

Published by Island Moonlight Publishing
New Zealand and Hawaii

www.islandmoonlight.com

For inquiries, contact the publisher:
info@islandmoonlight.com

National Library of New Zealand Cataloguing-in-Publication Data

Mete, Val, 1938-
Growing up a Chatham Islander : on the edge of 44 degrees South / by Val Mete.
ISBN 978-09677253-8-3
1. Mete, Val, 1938- —Childhood and youth. 2. Chatham Islands (N.Z.) I. Title.
993.99–dc 23

This story is dedicated in memory of cousin
Charles Cedric Preece
1940 — 2011

We played, we fought and that was us, whilst growing up like the wild flowers of Rekohu.

Contents

Author's Preface   vii

Foreword   xv

Owenga   1

Whanau   5

Life on Chatham Island   11

Horses   17

Other Ways of Getting Around   23

Gardens   29

Fishing Industry   35

Peat Fires and the Clears   43

Wild Cattle   46

Kaimoana   49

Father   57

Being Children   63

Communication   73

Wash Days   76

Home Remedies   79

Trading and Shops   85

Kai, Kai, and more Kai   89

The Weather   100

The Whale   103

Other Activities   107
Our Culture   111
New House   113
Other Delicacies and Cooking Methods   117
Tree Carvings   123
More Memories   125
Grandma and Grand-dad   128
The Races   133
School Days   139
Attending School in Napier   143
Our Last Trip Home   149
Cropping the Islands   156
Personal Footnote   161
Author's Statement:
What it means to me to be Moriori   163
In Appreciation   167
Family Photos   169
Recipes   176
Glossary   180

Author's Preface

This is a personal story about my childhood years on the Chatham Islands, also known as Rekohu and Wharekauri, which lie to the east of New Zealand. The Islands were known as 'Rekohu' by the Moriori (the indigenous people of the Chatham Islands), probably because of the misty skies under which they lay. 'Wharekauri' was what the Maori (the indigenous people of New Zealand) called the Islands. The first European sighting of the Islands was made from the Tender called HMS "Chathams" in 1791, thus the reason for naming them the "Chatham" Islands.

The Chatham Islands are an archipelago located in the South Pacific Ocean at S 44° W 178° and about 860 kilometres east of Christchurch, New Zealand. They include two inhabited islands. The larger, called Chatham Island, consists of approximately 90,000 hectares and the smaller Pitt Island is about 6,327 hectares.

One of my reasons for doing this book was to collate the memories of my childhood and put them into a story. I do get tired of reading about the same old history that seems to be copied from somebody else's writings. I don't intend to go there — by that I mean, I don't want to write about 'the invasion' or anything to do with the Moriori / Maori wars. I want to share all my precious memories of what it was like to grow up there from the late 1930s to the early 1950s. Forgive me if I'm a little inaccurate. This is a story about *my* life whist growing up on Rekohu / Chatham Islands.

A few years back, I started jotting down the odd story or two pertaining to my childhood days, all in easy language suitable for young children. These stories are not written in chronological order, therefore events aren't written in order of occurrence. I had originally arranged for my friend to translate them into Maori [Ngati Mutunga dialect] and my daughter to illustrate, and then my intention was to donate a booklet to Te Kohanga Reo o Wharekauri – Chatham Islands. My main aim then was to introduce the food of our islands to the children of the 'Maori language learning nest' of the Chathams: *nga tamariki o te Kohanga Reo nga kai o matou kainga–te motu o Rekohu / Wharekauri*. Thus I began writing my memoirs about *nga kai o mai ra ano* (the seafood especially from earlier times) plus the harvesting, preparation and presentation of such.

I left writing my memoirs in abeyance for a few years, but still had the desire to continue at a later date. In time, however, after thinking about some of the Chatham Island documentaries I have seen, and having had questions asked of me about certain things from the older days, it spurred me on to put ink to paper. More and more I appreciate some of the old ways, and it saddens me to think that some of this knowledge is being forgotten and lost forever.

One particular TV documentary that I recall was about hunting and killing *weka* (an edible bird). Compared to how we used to do it, the process was gruesome, to say the least. We certainly didn't whack the *weka* against a post and then wring its neck. That poor *weka* would have been as tough as an old boot. Instead, if you use a bird dog, it will bring the bird to you alive. Then you feel it, and if it's fat enough, you squeeze its heart to kill it. If it's too young or skinny, you let it go again. In practising this method, the *weka* will be tender as a chicken. Many of the old ways were very clever and effective.

I notice that tourists and TV crews really want to see the way that 'born and bred Islanders' do things, e.g. their *tikanga* and *kawa* (customs and protocol) exercised. Don't get me wrong, I'm not trying to tell you how you 'should do things.' But when someone who wasn't born or even raised on the Chatham Islands takes over and then says, "this is how 'we' do it on the Chathams" ... well I think it would be more appropriate if a Chatham Islander hosted these media events or told the stories.

I will give you an example. A group of tourists visited our home village of Nuhaka, NZ, and they wanted to see a *marae* (tribal meeting house) in action. There are six *marae* here. They weren't wanting to go to our big and newer community *marae* – the Kahungunu Marae. No, they wanted to visit our oldest marae, the Manutai, which is over 130 years old, and see how the people did things way back then. That is authentic cultural history, and that is what interested visitors want to see.

I too enjoy watching the Tuuta *whanau* (family) hosting, as well as the Day and Prendeville *whanau* and Pita Thomas. The way they use the old methods of smoking *kai* (food), using the old-time smoke-houses fired with rotting *kopi* with smoke smouldering at the right velocity, and still adhering to our Island *tikanga* that were passed on by our Elders.

Mind you, to be fair, I do realize that change is progress, but I feel it's got to be a change for the best. I find it so hard to look and listen to someone who has only lived there for a short time and then say, "This is the Chatham Island's way."

I also feel that if the Island child of today or tomorrow does not have any written stories about how we survived prior to regular shipping and flights to and from the Islands, they will never know, unless their Nannies have told them. In today's world, most of our children on the Islands, as well as here where I live now in Nuhaka, are not even aware of a lot of edible foods from the *moana* (sea). For instance, some of the most gruesome looking creatures from the ocean are actually the most succulent morsels to the palate. I hope the *tamariki* (children) will gain some knowledge from these tit-bits I share, and at the same time whet the appetites of the more senior citizens of the Islands.

After discussing my desires and thoughts on all this with several people, they encouraged me to change my direction and develop my stories into a more comprehensive book, which I have done. But before continuing, I'd like to tell you about my very beginnings, and why when I do write or speak, it is with a purpose.

Probably the most personal hindrance in my early childhood was having a speech impediment; I was unable to pronounce most words until I was about six years old. I had my 'pet names' for everyone: Eileen was Ninny, Charlie and Cissie were Tarly and Titty, and school was 'cool' just to name a few. One old lady down the road said I was simply 'tongue tired' and another said I had a 'short tongue.' I was quite confused, which didn't help matters.

At school the older kids often persuaded me to climb up onto the slide in playground and deliver my rendition of 'You Are My Sunshine.' It must have been as funny as a play because it created a lot of laughter and clapping. They made mirth of my impediment, and I honestly can't say whether I felt important or whether I felt like a clown!

In later years I felt sad about my circumstances because I realised that I would have missed out on the most important time of learning — the 'grounding process' or the drilling in the fundamental subjects when I first started school. I could *understand* but I couldn't express myself, and I often thought, "I can't be 'dumb' because I know how to 'do' things." At least I wasn't thrown to the back of the room as a 'special needs' pupil.

Fortunately, when I was about six years old, metamorphoses kindly took over and I began to speak and read. I got a grasp on pronunciation and the phonetic system, and life became more exciting, and of course it helped with my character building. From then on I have always believed that 'listening' is one of the greatest ways to learn. Even though I could not talk properly, I must have 'listened' to a degree, because it was quite a smooth transition for me.

The impediment did leave me with an inferiority complex for sometime. However, I have over time manifested evidence in self-assertiveness and have become a free spirit. I am truthful, thoughtful, punctual and if I am unable to fulfil my obligations, I would certainly notify those concerned. I guess my determination to emerge out of that place I was trapped in has intensified my view on life.

I am so 'in love' with nature and the beauty of our Islands, which are well-known for the endemic bird and plant life. We have the Chatham Island black robin, tomtits, shags, molly-mawks, warblers, snipes, oyster-catchers, *taiko* (petrels), *titi* (mutton-birds), parakeets, pigeons, shore plovers, the northern royal albatross, and others. These days the Department of Conservation takes care of the birds, endemic flora and fauna on both main islands, as well as the outlying islands.

On Chatham Island there are several lakes, and the huge Te Whanga Lagoon covers approximately 72 square miles. The lakes teem with food such as eels, flounders, white-bait, cockles, swan, and duck, and the sea and rocks are abundant with fish and shellfish.

I grew up in Owenga and seldom ventured any further than beyond Waitangi, and that wasn't until a couple of years before coming away to secondary school. I didn't know much about the rest of the Island or what it even looked like. I presume that the reason for not having gone to other places was because of inadequate roading. The only way to travel those days was by horseback. The men folk got around. They could take shortcuts by riding through the lakes on the right tides, etc. In fact, they seemed to enjoy it. Now the roads are accessible and the four-wheel-drives can trek anywhere, making the Island more suitable for the tourists and the locals as well.

For those who are not familiar with the Chatham Islands, Owenga is situated on the southeast coast of the Island. We were sort of 'out on a limb' until the roads were developed. Pitt Island lies about 17 kilometres southeast of Chatham, with Owenga being the closest port. There are a number of outlying Islands mainly in close proximity to Pitt Island as well as rocky outcrops.

I haven't had any previous knowledge of storywriting, especially for a published book, so this being my first attempt, I hope you will be able to decipher my written impressions. I have enjoyed gathering these memoirs and photos over the years, and I truly hope you will enjoy all of them. Finally, these stories are not fiction, they are a true rendition of my childhood life at Owenga, Chatham Island.

'Mum' and 'Father'
— Lily (Riria Riwai) Preece
and Charles Henry Preece, Senior

Foreword

Valerie was born on the Chatham Islands, which are known as Rekohu by our ancestors, the Moriori. She lived on the Island until she was in her 14th year, and then went on to secondary school at St. Joseph's Maori Girls College in Napier, New Zealand.

She descends from two Moriori ancestors — namely Riwai Te Ropiha and Kiti Karaka [Clark]. Kiti was also of Ngai Tahu descent, this being her Moriori / Ngai Tahu side. On her father's side she descends from the Black whanau of the Chatham Is. Val's mother was Mate Preece, my sister, and Val was her first born before she married John Harvey with whom she had a large family. Val was also her grandparent's first grandchild and was immediately adopted by them at birth [Lily and Charlie Preece], thus growing up as Valerie Preece and believing that they were her real parents. She was never told anything different. She loved her parents dearly, and their love for her was also boundless. She was spoilt by all of us. Mum Lily died when she was only four years old, and father, Ngaria [Lily's sister] and I brought her up with help from the family until it was time for me to come away to Christchurch for work. By then Val was old enough to help around the place.

Ngaria Martin nee Riwai.

There is seven years difference between Val and I. After the Second World War, when brother Bunty [Alfred Preece Snr] returned from serving in the 28 Maori Battalion, he married Myrtle Hough, and after a wee while he dismantled our old house and built a new one. Then Val and father stayed with them.

After her schooling, she went teaching as a JA at the Whakaki School, a short distance from Nuhaka in northern Hawkes Bay. It was during this time that she met her late husband Paul Mete. Val also worked at the Nuhaka Post Office on the telephone exchange, and then at the Freezing Works in Wairoa for over 20 years as a Customer Service and Quality Control Inspector. During her time there she worked for three different companies – Swifts, Waitaki Industries and Affco.

Because of the onset of arthritis, she took voluntary redundancy from Waitaki and then went onto the relieving staff at Wairoa College. Val took leave from College in 1998-1999 to go to the Chatham Is. to cook for the builders during the initial stages of the erection of the Moriori Marae, this being her *koha* (gift) to her Iwi. I do believe that was something she would never want to go through again. Even though it was great for her to be home, the job was very trying. "A job from hell" she said. She told me, "to come back to Wairoa College was just a breeze and a joy to be back in a more normal, organized and happy working environment." After retiring, she did a lot of catering on the big Kahungunu Marae in Nuhaka. This was her forte up until recently.

Val lost her husband in a road accident on Anzac Day, 1983, and has been a widow since. They have three adult children, six grandchildren and six great-grandchildren.

She has always had a passion for putting pen to paper. She tells me she has always been inspired to write about her young days because of her habitual urge to reminisce about the people who populated her thoughts and are still very much alive in her memories, as well as being a record for her children and their children.

Rain, hail, sunshine, wind, dust or mud — the Chatham Islands will always be her piece of paradise.

I hope you will enjoy reading this book.

Eileen W. Soanes, Napier.

Bunty and Myrtle while on their honeymoon in Rotorua, late 1940s.

Val Mete shelling paua, about 1984.

Owenga

During occasions in the past when I have been fortunate to go back to the Chatham Islands and roam around my old haunts, I can't help but reminisce about my childhood and growing up around the beaches and rocks of Owenga, my home town. I went so often to get *kaimoana* (seafood) for the elders by myself ... I can still remember every pool and where all the *kaimoana* virtually sunbathed during the low tides. Sometimes my Nan wanted only four or five *paua* (abalone) — just enough for cooking that day.

When the wind was okay for fishing off Louis Rock, the elders would often request only two blue cod — mainly for the heads more than anything. On those days, the hook and line would be ready for me as I arrived home from school. Our 'supermarket' back in those days was the ocean and land itself, something I remember and treasure greatly today.

After settling in Nuhaka, in upper Hawkes Bay on the north island of New Zealand, I have been back to the Chathams several times during my life. My late husband Paul and I went back to live for just over three years in 1968-1971 with our three children. Again, I am happy for having those three short years there. Our kids will always cherish their precious time there. Somehow the experience just added an extra string to their bows. It's something they can refer to throughout their lives. The 'island scene' fitted their fantasies during that period of their growing-up. When they hear someone speak of the Chathams, they sidle-up and say, "I've been there." Yes, if I won a lotto tomorrow, I would take all of them and all the *mokopuna* (grandchildren) back for a holiday for a month or so. That may satisfy all of our dreams.

I am writing mainly about Owenga because this was and still is my *turangawaewae* (spiritual home) or my stamping ground. When I was young and living there, I knew little about the rest of the Chatham Islands. Other parts of the main island, named 'Chatham Island', have their own characteristics and uniqueness of landscape; beaches, lakes, forests, birds, creeks and rock formations, types of harbours, soil colour and 'coca-cola coloured water creeks', to name a few.

One of the most interesting features of the Chathams is how they differ from place to place. For example, it's amazing how the red bluffs around the Petre Bay in Waitangi attracts attention from the Main Store or from the ANZ Bank and Post Office, as this is where one gleans the best view of these defiant looking cliff-faces. On a calm day they take on a serene image, but during a rough sea they stand there with a vengeance as the gigantic white-capped waves smash against their feet. It's interesting how when living on an island, the weather dominates its very soul, plus the plants as well as the bird life, and last but not least, the fish, animal and human inhabitants as well. A lot of the island prosperity depends on the abundance of the sea, and when *tawhirimatea* (the wind) rears its ugly head – it all turns to custard.

The rock pools in Owenga are quite different from other areas. And the soil in Owenga is rich and black and nourished with peat, ideal for gardens. When approaching Waitangi from the South Coast, one captures another sight of another lot of the spectacular red cliffs as they dominate the view. They are quite majestic. In Owenga there is only one red cliff — this being the point jutting out between the two harbours, unfortunately not visible from the road, not that it matters I guess.

So you folks who know me will no longer wonder why I always make for these special places when I come back to Owenga. To tell the truth, it is therapeutic for me. Mind you all those little sojourns are now history, as I am rather 'arthriticky' now. Never the less, I am thankful for having done all those chores. I now can pass the knowledge on to my own *mokopuna*, as we are only a stone's throw from the beaches and rocks of lovely Mahia here in New Zealand. I have told them how they should respect the rocks and sea and the *kaimoana* that abounds within it — all the 'dos' and the 'don'ts' that I know our forebearers adhered to. These are part of my most profound and precious memories today.

Trawler and crayfishing pots on Owenga Beach.

Charles Henry Preece, Senior, in his beloved oil-skin coat.

Whanau

The 'Nan' I refer to in this booklet is Ngaria Martin nee Riwai, who was a sister to my Grandmother Lily [Riria Riwai] Preece. Everyone in Owenga called Ngaria "Honey". I believe it was because of her honey-coloured hair. She sort of automatically took over when Lily died and became my mentor in more ways than one. She taught me a lot of what I know about life skills pertaining to those days. Towards the end of her life she would call for me so often that eventually I attended to her and Jack Pa, her husband, every day after school. I consider myself lucky to have had such precious time with these two Karapuna / Tipuna (ancestors, elders). They both passed over within days of each other, the year before I came away to school. At the same time Aunty Eileen, Aunty Myrtle and Aunty Cissie were also my minders.

But Father was my principle minder, and whatever he said was "carried" as his word was lore where I was concerned. Father (actually my grandfather) was Charles Henry Preece, Senior, and he was of Welsh decent. A young man when he arrived on Chatham Island, he grew up in Christchurch on the South Island of NZ.

One of many gifts he possessed was the skill in pronouncing Maori and Moriori words. I could have learnt so much if only I was more interested at the time, but I suppose it was the same with many children. In saying that, there are certain things that have imbedded in my mind; they are the very fundamental life skills. He respected the lore or erudition of the sea and the land. When harvesting *kaimoana* he warned us never to throw any offal back into the sea, meaning back into the pools where we shelled our food; that would eventually send the live ones out of those pools that were being affected by fouling them up. Unfortunately not everyone adhered to that *kawa*. I must add that the last time I went to that same place the *paua* had been depleted and those that were still there had moved further out to the deeper pools. The same thing is happening all over. We used to be able to gather food on a half tide, and grab a crayfish to boot.

I certainly abide by these rules here when we go to the rocks; I respect Tangaroa (God of the sea) and the *kawa* of this place. Our ancestors always recited *karakia* (prayer) before going fishing – in fact there was *karakia* before embarking on any venture. I shudder when I see these rituals being lost.

When I left the Chathams to go to College in Napier, Aunty Stella Cotter became my Guardian during those years. She also taught me so many fundamental principles to do with life here in the Mainland New Zealand. Aunty Stella was the daughter of Nanny Ngaria and Pa Jack, and lived most of her life in New Zealand. She and Uncle Charlie did go back to the Island for a year or two after their first son was born. They lived with her parents and while they were there, their second son was born on Chatham Island. Their home is in Rangiahua, just out of Wairoa in northern Hawkes Bay, and this is where I spent most of my holidays while away at St. Joseph's Boarding School. Isn't it amazing how one's whole lifetime is a learning curve? I give thanks for having all of these people in my life.

Living here in Rangiahua with this side of my New Zealand *whanau* gave me an extra dimension to my life after leaving the

Chathams. While Maori (the native language of New Zealand) was a compulsory subject at College (high school), I learnt more about *tikanga* and *kawa* living amongst the loving people of that place. All the Nannies were so real, genuine and loving, and I soon felt like one of their very own *mokopuna* (grandchildren). Nanny and Nanny-Pa Cotter [Stella's inlaws] were the most awesome people I have ever known. I still find solace when I go back for family functions. In fact I enjoy going back there to *karakia* (pray) occasionally, and to share a meal with *whanau* afterwards. This Maori sub-tribe of Ngati Kahungunu is Tama-Te-Rangi, and they are a very gentle and modest people. I also felt nurtured by those elders during my adolescent years — a big bonus for someone so far away from her home.

Aunty Stella Cotter

I finally made my own home in Nuhaka, just north of Wairoa in Hawkes Bay, after marrying Paul Mete, my late husband. I have lived here for 55 years in our own home, and I

Pa Jack and Nanny Ngaria

can not go any further without acknowledging the people here as well. I'm sure if it weren't for these folks and the way they have embraced me into the community, I would have been gone from here by now. Again, I was treated with respect and nurtured by the older people and nourished with all the *kawa* relating to this local environment.

I was a young 19 year old woman when first arriving here. Paul and I went to all the functions at our local *whanau marae* (family meeting house) down the road, and that was another learning curve. I was so shy, young and naïve, and not used to seeing so many Maori in the same place at the same time, most of them speaking Maori at that. I knew enough to know they were often talking about Paul and me, and of course it was all fun, as they enjoyed seeing me blush. I now wish they were here with us today, knowing what I know now. These were wonderful days.

However, to cut (what could become) a long story short, I also loved these old people who have all passed on now. They moulded me into the Nuhaka person I am today – a part of the Rakaipaaka Iwi, the local sub-tribe of Ngati Kahungunu. I must confess that I have planted my roots here. I'm also fully aware that I do not have any blood connections here. I know my *whakapapa* (ancestry), but my children are Rakaipaaka and Ngai Tuhoe through their father Paul.

Mind you one would think I *whakapapa* to here, as I have held many positions and do a lot of decision making on the committees on which I sit and convene. There are people here, the same age as my children and older, who really do assume I am of Rakaipaaka descent. I appreciate their thoughts, *but* I could never falsify or fake my *whakapapa* to suit circumstances. I am thankful to the people here for the way they *awhi* (embraced) me.

Whanau 9

Pat Preece and Aunty Myrtle, mid 1980s.

St. Barnabas Church in Owenga.

Life On Chatham Island

How I cherish my childhood memories... especially gathering *kaimoana*. Some times I would have to bring a lot more *paua* home for my birth mother and the rest of our *whanau*. And the *paua* was huge! My extended family lived directly across the road from Nan, a 2-minute walk. To carry the *paua* home I had a piece of wire that I threaded the *paua* on (poking the wire through the centre white part) and then bending the wire to form a circle. So much easier to carry, and one could carry heaps this way. Of course the old folk, Father included, insisted we take the seafood offal and shells up onto the dry sandhills. I used to wash the *paua* by swishing them in the pools when they were securely on the wire.

Other days the Nans would want watercress, and this had to come from the creek at the Brook where the water flowed swiftly. They were both sick and only wanted a taste of these foods. Then when the *kopi* berries were ripe and soft, I had to go to the Brook again to pick them from a certain tree up in the small gully. Consequently, I learned how to prepare these for consumption as well.

By the way, the 'Brook' was a family farm property which is now owned by cousin Alfred Preece. The original name of the property was 'Waiakana' and the Oldies always referred to it as that. It got the name Brook because an Uncle of ours lived there in the 1930s and his English wife thought the creek trickling down past their house resembled a wee brook, hence the name. There were three houses standing there when I was young. The Smiley family lived there before moving to Kaingaroa. They had seven boys going to Owenga School.

Several people lived close to the lakes and the lagoon where there were several sheltered bays and inlets and floundering posies. They would have done a lot of swan-egging and white-baiting and floundering and eeling on the lakes, making boats and sailing them on the lakes. Others at Kaingaroa had the beautiful white sandy beaches, bushes and rocks, the Weizner Brothers' exotic fruits and flowers, and then there was the Seal Colony at Te Whakaru as well.

The people living up the South Coast were blessed with their places of interest, like native bush and endemic plants and birds. They have rocks that are so abundant with seafood on a low tide, as well as the blue-cod that are so trapped in the pools when the tide goes out, that they jump onto the dry rocks and almost into your lap. This isn't a figure of speech or an hyperbole – this is a fact. I have seen it with my own eyes. About twenty-something years ago, Uncle Charlie had permission to go through the paddocks to the rocks – it was amazing. I am pleased that it is on private property. That was the place where we literally sat on the dry rocks and picked our *paua* out of the pools, and only our hands got wet.

There are lots of equally interesting spots. I have never been to Waitangi West or Wharekauri or any of those places along the top of the Island, so I really can't comment. However, I must say I went with Uncle Riwai and Oscar Johansen to a place called Waihi to visit Old Mr. Moffit some twenty odd years ago. What a lovely sheltered haven where the house is. They had grapes growing there, and this is what I mean about having shelter, because then you can grow whatever, as the soil is great in most places. I particularly liked the driveway going up to the house with the arbour of *kopi* trees on either side with masses of lovely Chatham Island lilies flourishing underneath these trees.

My Nans and Mrs. Nielson were great workers for our church, St. Barnabas Church in Owenga. They worked tirelessly and fundraised continuously for the up-keep of the building. We all worshipped together regularly and I can still see the lovely yellow crocus flowers that Mrs. Nielson put in the church during the months of spring. The Catholics celebrated Mass in the school on occasional Sundays. Aunty Myrtle cared for the Priest, and he stayed with us whenever he stayed over.

The Nielson house is still standing proud on the hill in the middle of Owenga. I have always said that it has the best view in the village. I was pleased to see that it is being cared for, renovated and extended. Directly across the road down in the paddock is the Hill family's old home, which has also had several changes. Friends of mine now own it and they love their hacienda. On my last trip home, they had a flourishing garden and a massive crop of potatoes.

Next door to this place is Tom Suvich's old house which is now owned by a local person. Then up on the hill by the cutting is Bob Jacob's old house. This house was originally owned by one of our uncles in the 1940s. There was no one in it at that moment. We lived there in about 1947 while waiting for Uncle Bunty's new house to be completed. Its also good to see that this house that was once Uncle Bunty's is still well and alive. Uncle Charlie's house is also in its same place in Owenga. The current owners have done great renovations here. And of course there's the Owenga Station Homestead still standing majestically on the rise, the only two-storied house left in Owenga, and Uncle Bunty resides there. The rest of the houses in Owenga are relatively new compared to these older ones.

I sometimes rode to Waitangi with Aunty Myrtle and Uncle Bunty [a 14 mile ride from Owenga]. We always called into Aunty Nora and Uncle Wilfred's place for a comfort stop as well as a cuppa. I loved calling in there because Annie and I played on the piano. This place was called "The Bar Twenty" or the halfway house. Aunty Nora was Aunty Myrtle's sister, and hospitality simply oozed out of her. This place was a stones throw from the quarry so it was a breather before continuing on past that place. Many years later, when she had retired to Christchurch, I went with Aunty Eileen and Uncle Athol to visit her. The same warmth and homeliness exuded there.

It is a fact: if you are a Chatham Islander now living elsewhere it makes no difference to our old habits; Island hospitality still prevails. Aunty Eileen who now lives in Napier does exactly the same, the kettle is always 'on the boil' so to speak. She just loves having visitors; Bless them.

Our Nan was exactly like that. I have been told that on a fine weekend she packed up a whole heap of food and then gathered up all the children in the village, harness up the bullock team and away they went to Shelly Beach [about two and a half miles away] for a picnic. Some of the older ones rode their steady steeds and also carried some gear. We often went along there on the Chatham Island race days before the formation of the roads. We played in the Te One creek [no connection to the place of the same name], hide and seek in the bushes and on the beach around the big rocks. When the fire was lit the kerosene tin was put on to cook the *kotutu* (boil-up) in. The adults would call for us to go and collect our eating dishes off the beach. These were huge *paua* shells that used to wash up during a rough sea and left high and dry amongst the other shell up on top of the beach. They were a common sight then, and some were as big as porridge bowls. We washed the sand out of them in the sea until they were fit for a King to eat out of. They were a dime a dozen those days and we really didn't take much notice of them. Now one that size would only be accessible if dived for.

While we were playing, the adults were gathering *paua* and *taere* off the rocks, probably with their shoes on. You could get them about a few feet off the shore at low tide. *Taere* were a small mussel like a *kutai*. They were cooked on a hot plate over the embers, they didn't require too much heat. The *paua* were sat directly onto the embers in the shell. I don't know if many have seen a *paua* cooked in this manner, but it does the neatest twist without falling out of its shell, and turns its 'sunny side up' virtually by turning itself up-side down. Great to watch. And they are as tender as can be.

Even though we were surrounded by water and the sea, we didn't play too much in it. Very few of us really knew how to swim properly. Weather permitting, we always went somewhere for a picnic prior to the formation of the main highway. Anything or anywhere was better than being at home. Fortunately we all enjoyed one another's company. No one did anything in Owenga without the whole village knowing. Sometimes I wonder if it was caring or just being downright nosey!

Cousin Charlie rode several winners, circa 1963.

Horses

As I approached Standard 5 and 6 (about 12-13 years old), I was finally old enough to ride a horse to Waitangi (our main township). Horseriding was the 'in thing' at that time. My horse was called 'Magpie' I think she was named that because she was a black mare with white on her face and a fluff of white on her fetlocks. Sometimes I left quite late to go back to Owenga, and darkness would befall us. My horse was so clever that in the dark she knew where every ditch or hazardous place was. I only had to loosen the reins and let her go, she knew how to jump all the drains. The roads were only partially formed, but not consolidated. Father never worried about me as he knew Magpie would bring me home safely. It was quite neat on a moonlit night with weka darting here and there and squealing and squeaking as if to say; what are you doing in my territory. Father was not in favour of un-harnessing a horse as soon as you arrived home. He preferred to let it cool down before taking the saddle off, and then he would groom the horse before letting it go. He really knew his game when it concerned these lovely

My sisters and brother, circa 1952.

faithful equines. I was never afraid of the wild cattle when riding because they were more scared of the horse and scampered off into the wild clears when they saw us coming.

Horseriding was the only mode of transport prior to and also during the 2nd World War. If one was lucky enough, you also owned a jogger. This was a cart-like vehicle with two pneumatic tyre wheels, seating about six people, usually three adults and three children. Two horses were attached to a shaft which was then attached to the collars of the horses. Joggers and drays were popular modes of transport. A dray was much bigger than a jogger and mainly used for heavy cartage. I never saw one used for transporting people, although they could have done so in other parts on the Island. The dray sat up high off the ground as it had big wagon-like wheels and seemed to have more spring in the chaste – something like you might see in a Wild West movie.

We also drove sledges pulled by bullocks. I was quite a dab hand at harnessing or yokeing-up the team, and sometimes one bullock was enough, depending on the weight of the load. I was taught by Father who was the best teacher, as he was a master horse handler as well as good at caring for other animals. He was also an excellent race-horse trainer, and in his day he worked in Coutts' Stables in Riccarton. Incidentally, Uncle Riwai followed in his footsteps and worked in the same Stables for years before returning back to the Chathams.

'The cutting' was the opening from off the long beach of Hanson Bay onto the tracks. There were no roads then, and the tracks were only suitable for horses and sometimes sledges pulled by bullocks. In the winter these tracks turned into deep muddy quagmires in which even a horse could get bogged in, almost up to its belly! Often these tracks became impassable, and peat bog is extremely difficult to get out of.

On reflecting back to these times, I realise how lucky we were to have such good safe horses. Father trained and cared for these equines as if they were of the human species. He often said to me, "Horses have feelings too, and they all have their own characters." I found this statement hard to comprehend, as I hadn't at this stage realized his physiognomy — being able to see and visage.

When I first learnt how to ride a horse, he did his best to instil in me sound advice. The first job was learning how to care for the gear — this being the bridle, saddle cloth and saddle and the grooming gears. Then when catching a horse one needed to go about it quietly if that was possible; don't chase it around

Father with one of his horses, circa 1940s.

Draught horses about 1940.

Proud horse owners.

and around the paddock; that was teaching the animal 'bad habits'. *Aue!* A painful exercise to say the least. He eventually got the message through to me to calm down when approaching the 'mutt'. By now I had several names for the poor horse. His advice worked in the end.

Uncle Athol about to go swan-egging at Patiki Lagoon, circa 1950s.

The horses during that time were very scared of foreign sounds, like the sound and even the sight of a motor vehicle. When the Public Works started excavating at Sandstone [a quarry on way to Waitangi] to extract metal for the roads, they had bulldozers and other earth-moving machinery there as you would imagine. Well, what a nightmare trying to get your horse past that clamour of industrial din. She bucked and shied and went berserk with fear. I was more scared of 'coming off' in front of all those workers than anything else. Fortunately luck was on my side. Father had warned me to "keep a cool rein", and by this he meant not to let the horse know you are nervous because they feel the tremble through the 'bit' that is the part of the bridle that's in the horses mouth which is very sensitive and more so if you are pulling hard on the reins.

David Holmes with mailbags, late 1930s.

Other Ways Of Getting Around

In Owenga, the drays did all the carting, especially the wool bales out into the harbour to the waiting surf-boat. These boats took the bales to the ship moored out in the Bay. The reason for having to ship cargo from Owenga in this manner was because there were no roads between Owenga and Waitangi until about 1948, when the Public Works started the roading construction. The bales were rolled down the hill from the woolshed and then onto the beach, then onto the dray, and then out to the surf-boat. It was quite a 'sight' to see the big draught horses wading out into the harbour. The Owenga shearing shed sat directly above the beach in those days. Similar activity took place at Manukau, as well as other ports around the Island.

Boat days were always exciting times as it only happened once a year, or, if we were lucky, maybe twice. We kids always went to watch the process, even if it was during school hours. Our teacher was just as excited as we were. It was certainly a change from our daily routine. Of course there was a method in his madness – we wrote essays about "Boat Day" at a later date. We really made the best of our outings, especially whenever we experienced something out of the norm.

What made things more joyful for us is that we were allowed to jump from bale to bale and yahoo and carry-on. Such basic simple fun! I can't quite imagine children getting this much fun out of a simple activity like that today.

Father and Charlie next to our "tin lizzy".

My cousins and sisters with Charlie, John Harvey, Cissie, and Eileen, 1950s.

By 1949–1952 several people had motor vehicles. Uncle Charlie was the first one in our family to own a vehicle. It was a green "Model A" truck with a square cab and with all the bells and whistles of the day, lovingly known as "tin lizzy". We had many a happy ride on the back of her.

After the War and Uncle Bunty had been home for awhile, he bought a new car, an Austin A 40. That was pretty cool. Then the Harvey family invested in an Oakland car — a big green shiny automobile that was as solid as a rock with running boards and all. The roads were not very pleasant to ride over then because they were still being developed, and some places were quite tricky to negotiate. If it was fine, the dust was everywhere, and if it was wet and raining, there was mud everywhere. But you may know the excitement of riding in a modern vehicle that overshadowed everything else, even if we were crawling like snails. Time meant nothing and nobody worried about the conditions; no trains or buses to catch, so what the heck.

When the roads were partially developed, they later deteriorated over time, probably due to the insufficiency of suitable roading material. Local roading metal was so scarce and inferior at the time. They used shell and lime for surface material instead. They extracted lime from the Tuuta farm up past Te One called Te Marama. This was a huge quarry and is still visible from the main road today. But when bad weather prevailed, all turned to mud again. Later on a good quality metal was found on Whangamarino that is currently still used for roading. I have seen another quarry on the way to Kaingaroa. I think it is by the turn-off to Wharekauri Station. The last time home I saw something like a metal quarry on the Port Hutt road, but I forgot to ask the driver whether it was or not. However, the roads were great that time; no worse than any back roads here.

So to begin our trek to Waitangi we started by going down onto the beach near Te One creek, then over Shelley Beach. Along over the orchard paddock creek, I think the real name for this creek is Gillespies, then over another shallow creek called Kaiti then along to the cutting. Once into this territory one

Enjoying Eskimo Pies from the 'flying-boat' (seaplane) pilots and crew, early 1950s.

couldn't really say — hooray! We're now on "terra firma" no, one wouldn't be so lucky. Enter! You are now on the main highway to the rest of the Island, this was before any roads were made.

There was always a bridge over the Mangahou river in my time. When going to Te Awa Patiki / Hukurangi Point we simply rode up the long beach, constantly aware of what the tides were up to. If the tide was too high we rode along inside the dunes. The road from the cutting to the Mangahou was a nightmare to say the least. You had to cross the 'clears'. There were deep ruts like furrows left from previous sledge trips, but if one was on horseback you had a much better chance of fluking it!!. The track from there on was on much firmer ground, having no more 'clears' to negotiate.

These were some of the 'down sides' of living on the Chatham Islands. The generation of today would not realize the perseverance we endured. What amazes me is the fact that you never heard anyone complain. Perhaps it was because most of us knew no better. Today if the roads were like that I would be terribly 'stressed to the hilt' — *aue taukiri e!*

The year before I went away to Napier, the Sunderland Flying Boats started coming to the Island. Well, that was the beginning of another era, another door had opened. On plane days, the first thing we hung out for were the free ice creams that the crew brought over. They were 'Eskimo Pies' that they liberally dished out to the people. Having no freezer on shore was probably the reason they disposed of them very quickly. As I recall, the crew was so nice. I guess for them it was a joy to see the delight on the faces of all the children; it was like Santa Clause arriving.

About 1949 or 1950 New Zealand's Warship the "HMS Bellona" visited the Chatham Islands. She was on loan to the NZ Navy around April 1946 as an allied warship. We children from the Owenga school had the privilege of going on board. We were ferried out on launches to this massive grey ship anchored out in the stream, as it was too big to come up to the wharf. It was so high up out of the water that it was quite frightening climbing up the rope ladder. It wasn't easy getting from the launch onto that ladder, believe me. There were sailors sitting on swing-like things painting the sides of the ship, so we didn't want to make any 'slips' in front of them. Once on board we were given an extensive tour of the ship, after which we were ushered into their diningroom and given a light dessert of pineapple set in red jelly and drinks. We felt very important and thankful for the experience.

The Chatham Air Base was situated on the edge of Te Whanga Lagoon, and the planes moored out on the lake at Waikato Bay. Waikato Bay is a coastal bay on the western coast of the lagoon, but the area includes a sheltered site on the lake slightly inland, as well as the whole area around it. Regardless of whether it was a school day or not, everyone went to the Air Base. Our teacher had freight to collect as well. The huge orange buoy beckoned to the pilot as to where to drop anchor. It was a magnificent sight watching the flying-boat skimming across the water and then taxing up to its moorings. Boats similar to surf-boats were used to convey passengers and cargo — all the mail and freight to and from the plane.

These days often turned into picnics, especially if the plane was delayed. Islanders love picnics! Several sheds/buildings sat around here creating yet another outdoor ambiance. Cups of tea, sandwiches, cakes and scones were available if one should run out of time to make a picnic lunch. The thick bush surrounding this area formed a canopy, an ideal sheltered spot with the lake lapping on the sandy shoreline. It's not paradise here all the time, as you only need one hour of rain before everything turns to mud and slosh, but on plane days it was always calm because they wouldn't fly if the weather was inclement.

Most people ordered perishable goods, foods we were unable to have this fresh at any other time. One particular time I remember, our mother had ordered an apple box full of sausages and saveloys, a tomato box of tomatoes and cucumbers, a box of mixed fruit, and a big Belgium Sausage (the big luncheon roll they slice in the delicatessen section of the supermarkets today). All of us kids rode on the back of a truck on the way home (probably Uncle Charlie's truck) after picking up our supplies. You can imagine what we got up to on our way back to Owenga, since it took us about two hours. Yes, my brothers and sisters and I started nibbling at the fruit and saveloys. Quite a bit of it had been devoured by the time we arrived home, but luckily for us, nobody complained. If we were served only sausages and savs for Christmas Dinner, we would have been happy.

Someone did start up a sausage business in Waitangi — I think it was one of the Tuuta *whanau*, but it had closed before I came away. I remember them being lovely.

Gardens

My Aunt tells me that when they were young they'd cross the Hawaiki creek further up stream from Mr Guest's garden and sneak down to his strawberry patch and have a royal feast of fat juicy strawberries. Isn't it so true that stolen fruits are always nicer — even if they aren't ripe. What child never had this experience and excitement ... it was all part of growing-up.

This place was a sheltered haven in amongst the trees and shrubbery, and some where, some how, there must have been a fragrant shrub tucked away there that exuded a sweet aroma which greeted us every time. That scent lingers with me still. One might think I'm a little 'out there' but I found such beauty in all plant life. Sometimes I was scared to ask, "Oh, isn't that tree or flower lovely?"

Strawberries grew abundantly, as did gooseberries, currants, and elderberries.

Down in this same area by the creek grew a huge pussy willow. For those who aren't familiar with this tree, it has very few leaves. To me, its most prominent feature is the so-called flower. Flowers grow on long naked stems and the flower itself is most unusual, as it's like an oval shaped ball of fluff (about the size of a *kopi* berry). Well I often wanted to pick them like other flowers and arrange them in a vase, but I didn't for fear of being ridiculed by my mates. Even now I see beauty in every plant, and it bothers me not being able to have my own gardens like they were, with plants hanging down my bank on the roadside. I have come to realize that this was an integral part of my life and who I am, although I can no longer garden like I used to.

Some may find it hard to imagine strawberries growing to a huge size on the Chatham Islands where the weather forecast always sounds wet and gloomy, Believe me, it does rain, but it doesn't rain forever like one would imagine. If you have shelter you can grow anything. This area that I was talking about is one of the most sheltered places for planting. When we went back to Owenga for a holiday in the 1960s, Tommy Tuuta had the best and fattest strawberries I have seen, and they lived a stones-throw away from where Mr. Guest grew his patch many years before. We were staying at the Owenga Station and he would give Aunty Myrtle a mixing bowl full every other morning.

Mr. Guest also owned the two-storied house that stood beside the Hawaiki creek. The Pomare family lived in it. Aunty Grace Pomare was my Godmother. They came across from Kaingaroa to Owenga with a large family that boosted our school roll. Marie Pomare was my best friend. We saw each other recently ... She married Basil Hill from Owenga, and they now live in Tauranga, NZ.

We had our own vegetable gardens at school, and they were very productive. There were always fresh veggies to enhance the dinner table. We had our own favourites. Most of us enjoyed our peas, white snow-ball turnips, carrots and radishes. Some days when we didn't get around to doing our lunch, we simply munched on our own produce. We enjoyed the fruits of our labour.

We were awarded prizes for the best kept garden. As you know, it's simple to plant a garden, but it's a different story keeping the weeds at bay. With the soil being so fertile, it was a bonus for the weeds as well as veggies. We took great pride in our little patches, although having our own gardens wasn't too much of a big deal to us, because everybody had household gardens those days; it was a case of having to — a means of survival. When thinking back, anything you put in the soil grew. We grew quite a variety. Some people grew broccoli, curly kale, brussel sprouts and swedes, so with the soil being so fertile it was really rewarding, and a pleasure for the Oldies.

We thoroughly enjoyed gardening when Paul and I lived on the Island with our children. Everything grew like Jack's Beanstalk and it was great being able to supply the fish-factory (Ferons) and some fishermen with our lovely veggies. I even grew a long line of *puha* that just kept growing on and on — the more it was picked, the better it grew. We had peas that grew so quickly that they were bursting out of their pods. I could go on and on. Our garden ran along the side of Ferons between the road and the accommodation.

Father had a great vegetable garden, probably because he dug fish-heads, fish offal, crayfish bodies and *kina* shells into his compost, and sometimes seaweed as well. This beat any 'maxicrop'. There were no bought insecticides or fertilizers in those days, and you could virtually 'see' the stuff growing. It was unheard of for people to get veggies down on the boat. The Port Waikato [the coastal trader] or the Manuka, the other ship, were much slower than the ships of today. It normally took four to five days and sometimes more, to steam 'one way' and they didn't have the on/off loading mechanism they have today. Sometimes the boat sat out in the bay until weather permitted it to berth. We did get certain fruit, down on the boat, but they needed to be only half-ripe when leaving the shops. I think the population on the Island was more than it is today, and you now have a ship servicing the Island every ten days or thereabouts, and a plane nearly every day. The cost of living there is much higher for a lot of families than here in the mainland. The biggest disadvantage in cost is the air and sea freight. That is phenomenal.

We did our lawns with a push-mower at our school. There was a flowering currant tree by the front gate that gave off a distinct fragrance, the flowers were pretty pink clusters of bell-shaped droplets. There were also sweet-williams, marigolds, Californian poppies and others.

Nanny Ngaria and Pa Jack had another type of garden. They were the only ones in Owenga who grew sweet corn during my time, and they were lovely. Nan often cooked the cobs on top of the cabbage in *kotutu* (boil-up). They were aging by now, but they had these poppies that kept seeding down and popping up year after year (self-sown), which was a blessing, as they were past gardening by now. These flowers were of all colours and made a wonderful display across the whole frontage of their yard. They sure added colour to their twilight years.

Mrs. Jacobs (Amiria, Aunty Dolly's mother) also had a lovely garden at Manukau inside a hedge of flax. They managed Manukau at the time, and it was common knowledge that they ran that farm to its full potential. Incidentally, his grandson Abe is also a top Farmer. I watched that man working when I was cooking for the Moriori Marae builders while we were living in the next section to his Owenga property. I know how to sort the sheep from the goats. The Jacob's family were honest hard workers. Harold and Marge McClurg also managed the place. Then later in the sixties and seventies John and Hana Tuanui ran the place. We were living in Owenga at the time and were well aware that John was managing that place to the "max," another valuable overseer. We were all friends. Later after we had left I heard they had moved into the new house down the bottom by the road and that Hana had made beautiful terraced gardens; *Aue!* That was then. To me, flowers and shrubs enhance a property and gives it character as well as reflecting the character of the inhabitants.

There was a popular hedge that grew in Owenga, especially around the Donaldsons' house. We called it "kiss me over the garden gate." It has a dark green somewhat sticky leaf and pretty pink flowers. This also exuded a pleasing spicy aroma. There is a shrub of it down the road from me, I shall take a piece to the nursery one day and find its botanical name. Yes, I do have a 'love affair' with nature; flowers, shrubs, trees, endemic flora and fauna and vegetables. Even the lichen, mosses and the pink berries that grow in 'the clears' fascinate me.

Aunty Eileen and Aunty Myrtle sitting beside the garden.

Whole crayfish catch in early boom years, circa 1965.

Fishing Industry

Before the Second World War, the Blue Cod Fishing Industry was in full swing in Owenga. The paddock running parallel to the Hawaiki creek from the main road to the cliff above the beach, now owned by Nigel and Lou Ryan, was then called "The Company Paddock". This could have been owned by the Company during those lucrative years, probably how this place got this name.

I remember several houses occupying a corner of that paddock. These houses seemed to be clustered quite close to one another, mainly on and around a little knob. When the codding days were on the wane the paddock slowly became to look like a deserted gold-mining village, another place where we rummaged. Most of the workers moved on to other parts of the Island, most likely back to where they originally came from for work in the first place. However, during the codding days Owenga was thriving and the population of our village peaked at around 200. The freezer was situated directly across the road from where Mr. Guest lived, a short distance from the existing bridge.

Wood burning boilers provided the steam energy to drive the machinery. Imagine the cords of wood that had to be carted, but most of all the hard work the men must have had to endure in felling and then chopping, with no such implements as chainsaws those days. I guess the carting to the freezers would have been on a sledge with a bullock team pulling.

Old Mr. Prendeville was the Manager. He and his family lived in a big two-storied house in very close proximity to the freezers. I have no idea what happened to this house, but when I grew up they were living in another two-storied place on the hill [where Nigel Ryan lives today] and that was just down from where we lived. Unfortunately that house burnt to the ground. I remember seeing that fire. It was the most dramatic and scariest thing I had ever seen. The Prendevilles were milking cows at this time, as the freezers had long closed down, but after this unfortunate happening they moved into Waitangi.

There are still remains of the old Boiler there today. Nigel Ryan operates a crayfish factory there on the very spot. The shed is called "The Roaring Forties" and the factory trades under the name of "Maconee Seafoods".

During 1949-1950, Mr. James Jury [Jurivich], or Jim Jury as we knew him, came from Wellington and built a new fish freezer below the cliffs above the beach on Owenga Harbour. He and his wife and family settled in Owenga for a few years.

One very disappointing thing for us kids was the removal of 'our boat' the "Libya". This boat was a big stranded wooden trawler that sat upright against the bank for as long as I could remember. It must have been one raging tide that washed her up against that sand-bank. We had many happy times on our beloved wreck. She was so solid and even the wheel-house was still intact. Can you imagine the fun we had on her. There were too many Skippers and not enough deck-hands — similar to 'too many Chiefs and not enough Indians'. Yes, we fought for our positions on that boat. Eventually she had to go to make way for the new road that went through to make this big concrete construction. I suppose that was progress for a time. Fishing can be such a risky world — having to be ruled by the Sea God Tangaroa or the fickled moods of the sea.

Helicopter lifting crayfish for export, 1969.

During the crayfish boom in 1967-1972, this factory was literally alive with tonnes of crayfish crawling everywhere. This factory was now owned by Yovich & Hopkins from Hikurangi north of Whangarei. Like the other three factories in Owenga, Ascots, Ferons, and Skeggs, this was around-the-clock processing. The crays were pouring in all day from the helicopters who flew with full bins into the five sheds all day. There was no time to do anything with the 'body-meat' at that stage, as the commercial focus was exporting the tails. The 'crushers' (machines that crushed the shells into fine particles) often broke down under the pressure. When this happened, the bodies were carted and dumped up the back of the Owenga Station. A sad sight indeed, even though one was sick of the sight of them. I kept thinking of our *whanau* back home here, because most of those bodies had heaps of *kai* left in them. Deep down inside of me I felt guilt for having to dump *kai* like that, and 'fresh from the sea' to boot. But, that's how it had to be for awhile.

As the catch tapered off they started cooking the bodies and the meat was extracted. This provided work for the rest of the women in Owenga. I worked in the factory for a time doing this, and I was amazed at the amount of meat that we extracted from one body. We often averaged one kilo of weight from two bodies. In the early stages they used stainless steel pipes (called dongers) to smash the bodies. They brought women in from Yovich & Hopkins, Whangarei to teach us how to do the job. Everyone banged away in great style, and we were paid by the weight so there were heads down and tails up. Now they have extracting machines.

Unfortunately, in 1973 a violent storm reared its ugly head and the huge seas washed throughout the whole of the freezer, causing extensive damage to the generators and everything else in its path. The wrath of Mother Nature. The whole complex was pulled down after that. That raging rough sea must have been similar to the one that brought our boat the 'Libya' ashore.

Now going back again to the 1940s to the codding days of that era in Owenga, I know how arduous it was for that generation of fishermen. That was sheer hard labour. To earn a living from 'long-lining' must have presented several difficulties. Nevertheless, a living had to be made, and there weren't many other options. The wooden launches they fished on seem so small and inadequate when one surveys the remains of them today. They chugged along at a snail's pace when compared with the jet-boats of today ... although I have been told by an uncle that they were very seaworthy and actually quite comfortable to work on and even to sleep on. I believe him, but thousands wouldn't!

The preparations were still very exhausting and time-consuming. When the weather was unsuitable, the men busied themselves plaiting the hooks onto the lines. I remember helping Uncle Herbert to plait. I always enjoyed this because he was so neat to work with. No job was done good enough though unless it ended up perfect. He was a real perfectionist. I will never forget how to plait. In fact he and Aunty Nell were a loving couple, and they always reassured me on many of my attributes, something every child needs to be told. They weren't married when I first started helping with the hooks, but after they were wed, they still made me feel special. Then they went off to Pitt Island to live and farm, and I missed them terribly.

Towards the end of the 1940s to the early 1950s, codding was still the mainstay, allowing families to just survive. Some were fortunate in being able to supplement their income by running a small landholding.

After spending a considerable time at sea codding, some of the men were as 'dry' as wooden Gods, so their first port of call would be the pub in Waitangi. Sometimes one day turned into three days 'on the hops'. This would have been like a holiday, and of course there were no other options. After all, the women folk were quite capable of keeping the home fires burning. It was easier for those who had older children at home to help with the chores.

Considering the lack of amenities, the women were heroines, as this place was definitely a man's world. Not all mainland women were able to adapt or even like the Island lifestyle.

So while I write on about our happy childhood, it wasn't the same for everyone. I admit there were no outlets or deviations from the same ole mundane lifestyle – you just couldn't ring a friend and say "come on let's go to the café and have coffee" as you can now.

Sometimes during my childhood as I grew older I felt a little hard done by as I kept hearing of a different life beyond our shores. Now through a much broader and mature view, I do realize how fortunate I was to have grown up a Chatham Islander on our beautiful Island. But, in saying that, I have to reiterate again, it's not everybody's 'cup of tea'.

Around 1965 a new era began. Blue codding had declined as well as the prices for the fish. Fortunately, about this same time crayfish were discovered in droves, and was estimated to become a huge commercial venture, and fishing boats from

1968 — Daily dozens of these baskets arrived into each of the four factories in Owenga.

all over NZ were plying the Chatham waters like vultures in search of this lucrative crustacean. It was like a gold rush. This "Crayfish Boom" created a totally different lifestyle for a big percentage of the Chatham Islanders, with daily sales worth thousands of dollars in Owenga.

At the beginning there was so much crayfish, and the buyers were only wanting the tails. Several fishermen were 'tailing' at sea, and the bodies were tossed back into the water. Oh dear my heart bled to witness such annihilation. My mind went back to what our old people told me, "If you throw the offal back into the sea, the food will eventually disappear." Yes, they will venture off to safer grounds. In other words, it's a sign of greed with no thought of sustainability. This happened for some time, then eventually some buyers wanted the whole fish. Then it went back to tails only. Then the whole fish came into the factory, tailed, and the bodies were cooked and the meat extracted. This was a much better option. To see food wasted was criminal — mind you that's only my thoughts. Most didn't care because money was the important factor.

Believe me, time never stood still when a living was to be made. We all had to chip in and help. All the jobs I had to do were in order to keep the household running, especially when the men were out fishing for several days in succession. This was the year before coming out to secondary school. It was imperative that they made use of every suitable 'fishing day' because when bad weather set in, it could hang around for days. Looking back now I feel thankful (although I didn't then) for having learnt how to do all these things.

Father busied himself smoking blue cod and anything else that needed smoking, like bacon and ham. The smokehouse was a great invention. A big old galvanized water tank was open at both ends and set into place. At the bottom end a long trench was dug into place about six to seven feet in length. The fire was lit at the bottom end of the tunnel using wood that created a steady flow of smoke. Father used nothing else but rotting Kopi. He was adamant that this wood gave the food [especially blue cod] the best nutty flavour, and it smouldered slowly so as to smoke slowly and not cook the fish. There definitely is an art in smoking *kai*. They also smoked their own bacon, and it was very nice and never stuck to the pan like some of this fluid injected stuff does. In fact some bacon today is like it's artificial and seems like plastic. Unfortunately a lot of our food today is adulterated and diluted with additives, liquids and bulking agents. Corned beef today is injected with fluid and tastes nothing as good as when it used to sit in the brine for awhile – not as nice as when we did it in a brine in a wooden barrel and stirred it occasionally. Father smoked dozens of cod at a time. After hanging them on the bars in the smoker he covered the top with heavy sacks and let her go.

I remember when I was working at the freezing-works a friend of mine was intrigued with what he had heard about Chatham Islands, and he kept asking me questions like, "How big are the *paua* and *kina*?" "What about the size of the crayfish?" and a multitude of other questions. In the end it became quite embarrassing, as it actually sounded like I'd just come from Texas, where everything is 'bigger and brighter'! Yes, we were lucky to be able to live off the land and the sea. And our kids never got sick while we were there visiting or when we lived there.

The 'Clears' where the lichen and mosses thrive.

Peat Fires
And The Clears

The clears provided another favourite plaground. After a lot of rain (which was quite often) the ground became very spongy in places. We would delight in jumping up and down on these patches like they do on a trampoline today. We always discovered something new up in the wastelands. For one thing, the plants are delightful, and they are there thriving in their own natural habitat – the clears. I now realize why it is a botanist's dream to rummage around in them. My favourite plants are the ones with lovely little red berries that creep across the mossy floor of this peat land, plus the pretty delicate ferns that we often used for decorating purposes. The lichen and mosses are also interesting. A few years ago a group of people were harvesting that moss for export. They baled it up like a wool bale. I don't know what happened to that venture but I think the buyers used it for growing orchids in. This area was also a foraging ground for wild pigs and cattle, needless to say, we never ventured too far away from the residential areas.

It was a common sight, more so at night, to see the peat fires burning in the clears. These fires must have been burning forever. They were a fair way back from the village, and the flames were quite prominent, especially when the winds picked up. These fires were something we grew up with, so we were never scared of them.

Much of the land was covered in forest in the early days and, according to what we were told at school, one single species [Dracophyllum arboretum], commonly known as 'the grass tree', was the culprit for the peat fires. This tree grew up to 30 feet high, and had a short broad trunk from the top of which spreading branches grew bearing masses of erect needle-like leaves browny-green in colour with white hairy edges. (Sounds weird, doesn't it?) This tree burnt vigorously even when damp and this probably accounts for the disappearance of the forest. These peat fires continued over a wide area of the Island.

There wasn't so much surface conflagration, but there was steady underground combustion. Some of these fires went on burning for years; hence the wide-spread peat lands. As far as I know, today there are no visible signs of any fires like they were when we were young. There are many deep holes where these fires were; I guess they are all over-grown with fern and bracken. One would need to be aware of the where-abouts of these holes if venturing up the back country of Owenga and along the top of the Mangahou and Te Awa Patiki.

The places we refer to as the clears are the acres of land similar to the moors in Scotland and other places where there is heath and similar ground-hugging plants. All these peat lands are covered in bracken and native flora and fauna.

We often used peat in our stoves. Most households had the Orion stoves before upgrading to the enamel ones. Peat wasn't something we burnt too often, because it made the chimney sooty, and the heat was quite intense which was not good for the 'grates' in the stoves. However, it was good for a booster in small doses.

Every stove had a rack above it and some had a water tank and tap on the fire-box side, and this tank supplied hot water continuously while the fire was burning. We kept two irons on the back of the stove all the time for ironing clothes. The handles were kept on the rack. The rack had many uses, great for airing damp clothes, and when the fire was radiating a slow heat it was an ideal place to sit the bread dough to rise. We normally sat the bottles of home-made yeast on the mantelpiece. We covered our mantelpiece with news paper after cutting out pretty diamond and heart shaped patterns on the paper. Brown paper looked effective. The dry hops came in boxes; they resembled very soft flaky-like corn-flakes. The smell when the yeast was fermenting was like beer. When the cork flew out of the bottle, the yeast was ready to make bread with. This bread-making was a daily task for the big families.

Eventually, most households invested in Aga stoves, and then onto Diesel Drip. Now they have electric ranges, ovens and microwaves, bread-making machines, to name a few, in spite of the outrageous cost of electricity over there.

When I was young I learnt how to cook on a primus. This cooker was fuelled with kerosene and lit with methylated spirits, a handy implement to have to make the porridge on when the stove was hard to get going.

Around about the War years, wood was getting scarce so we had to use other burning materials. There didn't appear to be any replanting after felling so many trees for the Freezers. There were no trees immediately around us, except for a row of coniferous ones called macrocarpa down below our place. I'm thinking that perhaps old Mr. Prendeville may have planted them. We had lots of fun climbing them and looking for bird nests. Those very same trees are still standing, all twisted and gnarled with age. This row of trees runs along the back of Nigel Ryans. Over time when I've gone back to Owenga I look at those trees and the memories come flooding back. You can see them from the main road.

Wild Cattle

Those days all the roads in Owenga were in full use. There was what we called the "top road" [we lived on the beginning of it], the "bottom road", the two "side roads", and "the cutting" (this road runs down to the beach below Bob Jacobs' or onto Cloughs' beach, sometimes known as "down past Donaldsons"). Then there is "the brook road", then onto the "manukau race". Back the other way is the "freezer road", then the Owenga Station road, then along to "Shelly Beach". Owenga was quite a populated little village, and most of us rode horses all over these roads.

As kids we were scared of the wild cattle, especially at night when they would come right up to the boundary fence at the back of our house and roar, and the bulls would be rooting up the turf in a fury – so frightening. Somehow we fathomed out through listening to older kids that the cows were bully-ing, and it was during 'mating season' that this frenzy occurred. We would pull the blankets up over our heads to try deaden the sound of the wild raging animals.

Then later when my cousin Charlie (Aunty Cissie's son, to whom this book is dedicated) and I biked from Owenga to Whangamarino [just out of Waitangi] on our push-bikes after school on some Friday nights, we encountered another mob of these dreaded beasts that lived in the clears further on. We went as fast as our legs could peddle, especially when going along both sides of the Mangahou bridge where cattle poked their noses through the fern and rushes staring us straight in the eye and looking as if they were about to charge, with hot air exuding from their nostrils as they were snorting and working themselves into a frothy frenzy. This was immediately after the War, after they had built the bridge over Te Awa Inanga. Once we had crossed that divide we were safe, because the cattle were scared of the new bridge. Whew!! Our little hearts settled down to a normal beat.

Even though I am three years older than Charlie, he always beat me for anything physical. 'Young' Charlie and I were more like brother and sister, as we were the two first grandchildren, and spent a lot of time together with our grandparents Lily and 'Old' Charlie Preece. I don't think there was anyone who could beat my cousin in running or in any sport for that matter. He often left me behind in his dust on our trips across the divide. I would have to make out I was crying before he'd stop and wait for me. Whenever I hear the song, "Walk Don't Run." It always reminds me of Charlie, because I can't remember ever seeing him walk – he ran everywhere.

I was lucky to have a bike. Aunty Eileen and Uncle Athol had come home just after they were engaged for a short holiday. When they got back to Christchurch, Uncle Ath bought me a bike – he even had my name put on it. Well, when it arrived, I thought all my birthdays had come at once. Charlie got one too. I think we were the only ones in Owenga with them at that time.

Ben Coburn tailing his crayfish for export, circa 1984.

Kaimoana

To us the *inanga* is a delicacy; they are more like a big whitebait on the Chathams. We frittered them or cooked them whole in our homemade butter until they were nice and crispy ... yum. We also caught white-bait, *inanga* and flounders at the mouth of Hawaiki creek right where it runs into the sea. It was great fun spearing flounders. They were everywhere on the right moonlit night. Father knew precisely when to *"haere ki te mahi kai ika"* (meaning go and gather seafood). He knew the phases of the moon and judged the tides accordingly, and knew when the flounders were fat. We didn't need flounder nets — all we had were spears. They literally flapped around our feet, and we just took our pick, at the same time being careful not to spear our feet with excitement. We threaded our flounders on a number 8 fencing wire with a stopper on the end, and dragged them behind us.

There were certain moons for eeling as well. Hawaiki creek was the closest to home for eels, although I never went eeling in Owenga, I only eeled in the creek at Whangamarino. There didn't seem to be any need for us to go eeling because the menfolk always enjoyed that *mahi* (work). They would go up to the lake at Patiki, and while there they gathered all sorts of food. It was a change from fishing. Just riding a horse up the long beach was therapy, plus a bottle of 'whatever' to keep them happy.

I vividly remember Grandma Hough cooking us dried shark meat in the embers of the stove. The putrid smell permeated the air, I'm sure it must have been enough to frighten even the hungriest fly away. But let me tell you, the taste certainly overcame the smell. Once you got past the smell you were away munching.

Our Nans even dried *pipi* and *tuatua* to save going to get them during the winter months. They would throw them into stews. Picking *pipi* was another enjoyable event. First we harnessed our horses, prepared our *pikau* bags and rode off to the Long Beach/Hanson Bay. This beach is just on the outskirts of Owenga on the way to Waitangi. Yes, Father always knew the tides. We went when he said "the tide will be out for a long time today."

There were times when these bi-valves (see photo below) weren't so fat, but when the moon was in the right phase, they were plump and succulent. We enjoyed them raw, marinated in a sweet brine, made into fritters or in a chowder. You can do wonders with seafood and shellfish if harvested at the right time. After we had picked enough *pipi* shellfish (the hardest part was trying to squeeze your fingers between them, they were so plentiful), we played in the water, and this was great fun. We

sometimes lit a fire and cooked some on this old sheet of iron used on previous occasions, and had a 'tuck in'. Then back into the sea to wade out to the breakers, and by now the tide would be on the turn. Well we'd end up with mouths full of salty brine. After riding home we were tired and ever so thirsty. We drank copious amounts of water to try quenching our thirsts. It wasn't so much the *pipi* that made us thirsty; it was swallowing the salty water during all the frollicking.

I don't think many go along to get them now, so I suppose they are still there in abundance. Mind you, the folk won't eat the seafood unless it's 'fat', and one really needs to keep an eye on the moon and tides.

I had also witnessed the cod-gutting and heading in the factory in those days. These Gutters were in a league of their own, as this was also an art. The fish had to be processed soon as possible, probably because they didn't have ice on the boats. Pa Jack Martin was a champion Gutter. He had a thumb that looked like it was bent backwards. We were always intrigued with it; apparently it was the constant repetitive work that caused this. Today it is accessible for one to have a carpel tunnel syndrome operation to rid the throbbing pain, but those tough old fellows toiled and persevered with whatever was thrown at them.

But then the women were also martyrs in bearing the brunt of rearing and providing for the *whanau* under such circumstances. Yes, no fishing family was too much better off than the other, so we were all 'in the same boat' so to speak. If the boats were due in after school and all jobs were done we would sometimes go down to the harbour and watch the boats un-loading. The men with their fish bagged in sacks rowed them ashore in dinghies. There was no wharf those days. These fishermen had gnarled hands and weather-beaten faces that reflected a whole story of such sea-faring expeditions. Fishing today is a gentlemans' job compared to yester-year. Again that is all part of progress.

I must tell you about the 'square' holes in the bank of Te Awa Inanga. They were special holes, no doubt man-made, for catching *inanga*. Our Nannies made special *kete harakeke* (flax kits) and somehow lowered them into these cavities, and after a matter of minutes they'd pull them up and wallah!! Up would come a full *kete*, most of the time they'd have a mixture of *inanga* and white-bait. Nan Lily would take me along tied to her back while she was catching these things, or sometimes Aunty Eileen would have the honour of minding me on the bank. I was too young to witness this Island ingenuity. Aunty Eileen often went along and vividly remembers the excitement of it all. She also tells me that Nan carried me on her back everywhere she went, even when she was on the rocks getting *kaimoana*. Aue! I hope I wasn't the cause of her demise. "God bless her loving soul."

I remember being laughed at when eating *karengo* — known as *paieke* (sea lettuce) on the Island recently. As a child I collected and prepared it for the Nans. It is known as 'sea lettuce', a medicinal food as it is rich in iron, thus ideal for anyone with an iron deficiency. When it first appears on the rocks, it is a lush green colour, and when ready for harvesting, it has turned to a brown colour, and this is usually at the beginning of winter.

Someday some one like Roger Beattie will converge on the Island again, and start harvesting it, and make a fortune. The Japanese have been eating it for more than a hundred years. They use it as a food enhancer. They harvest it from here, take it back and process it into a powder or pressed into blocks, and they send some back here to sell through their Asian food outlets. I have also tasted it after being processed way back about 50 something years ago when my husband's cousin and his Japanese wife lived down the road from us. She sprinkled the dried seaweed into most dishes, the main one being my favourite called 'Suki Yaki' for extra flavour. You lucky Island people — you've got a gold mine at your front door.

Another point of interest is that we were taught to throw our first item of seafood — our first catch — back into the sea for Tangaroa [the God of the sea]. On the Chathams they call 'him' Maru. That is a traditional gesture of thanksgiving. Sometimes it was easy to forget these simple and basic rules, as excitement often overtook the rituals, especially when the first *paua* you clap your eyes on is a 'big' one, or your first *kina* was also tempting and hard to throw back. I over came this by looking for a small one and throwing this one back into the brine, this being my first catch. A bit naughty, aye?

Getting back to *paieke*, Nan often asked me to go gather some. When I collected it for the Oldies I had to get it from between Clough's creek and the Manukau race from a special rock there that has the thin stringy stuff. To us here in Nuhaka it is a delicacy; it's seasonal and we serve it with pride on our banquet tables. It resonates around the whole area when the first lot is harvested. Then everyone is 'hanging-out' for a feed. Not everyone can go get this stuff as one needs to go out to Portland Island [off Mahia] to gather it, and that means having to have a boat and the rights to go there. Like all seafood, one really needs to know how to cook it. Nan cooked it in the oven in a dish with a little water and a lot of butter for what seemed to be half a day or more. The longer and slower it takes to cook, the better. I can't wait when I cook it — I'm sampling all the time. Today with the invention of slow-cookers or crockpots, it's a breeze. Put *karengo* in with butter and let her go on slow temperature until soft and ready ... easy-peasy.

I like to gather different types of seaweed. My two daughters do the same. Janetta my girl who weaves has woven kelp, and Donna brought back a huge piece when she last visited the Island. She dried it and had it hanging outside in a sheltered place. Many people have not been able to guess what it is. She later discovered that you can't have it exposed to the elements, because any rain on it makes it go soft and out of shape and the hot sun is inclined to make it brittle. It is a great talking point, but by the same token, not everyone can see the beauty in it, however – *hei aha* – that's fine.

Talking about kelp, a lot washed up on Clough's beach in Owenga, I suppose because of the reef out in the bay off that beach. We would gather it and out of the big fat bull-kelp we made balls. We cut them round in shape with a knife and left them to dry, once they dried out you could bounce them. We also dragged the big wide kelp onto the hill and slid down on it. In this same paddock there was one certain place where there was clay in the bank of Clough's creek. We'd dig out what we needed and make our own marbles, take them home and 'fire' them in the oven. Our stoves were burning all the time, so the ovens were always hot. We also made brooches out of dough – baked them in the same way, and when cold and set hard, we had fun painting them. Imagine children having to make their own fun like that today.

When there was another certain wind coming in off the sea Father knew there would be this special kelp washed up on Clough's beach. He would say, "There will be plenty of *kaeo* on the beach today." In the Marine Book *kaeo* are called 'sea tulips'. We kids would go up and down the beach like mowers gathering these *kaeo* for the Elders. If it was an early morning tide during a school day, the Teacher didn't mind because it didn't happen very often, and we seldom had the right wind to wash these *kaeo* up onto the beach.

There must be a reef straight out from here where all this big kelp grows, and this must be a breeding ground for these morsels. Kelp grows in all its glory around the Island, but not all of it has *kaimoana* growing on it. Waitangi West is renowned for the *kaeo* at most times. We ate them straight out of their kelp cases, or marinated in a brine of water, vinegar and sugar, or battered like a mussel, or made into fritters. I do think that one needs to acquire the taste for these, and more so when you're young because they are a strong-tasting *kaimoana*. They would be one of my favourite seafoods. I can taste them as I write. To me they look like a long *poi*. The food case is sort of oval and this is attached to a long piece of kelp, like the string of the long *poi*. You split the case open and push the *kai* out with your thumb. But as I say, they are not everybody's 'cup of tea' or favourite nibble.

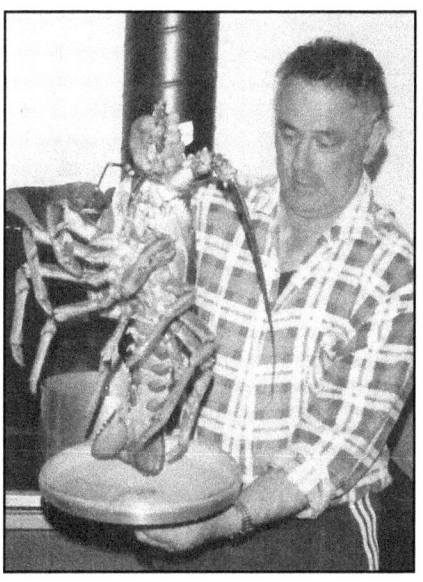

Charlie cooking a jumbo crayfish, circa 1986.

Father carted blue cod and groper from the beach to the freezer on his dray, taken 1930s.

Father

Father (Clarles Preece Senior) was so caring and loving, and always made sure that we were fed and clothed well. He loved me dearly and nurtured me from the day I was born. He was actually my Grandfather, as I mentioned earlier, and I adored him. He also had such a love for animals, especially horses.

I had never heard of the word 'diet'. Father was a stickler for feeding people very well ... part of Island hospitality. He made the nicest potato scones. There were always plenty of potatoes as they grew all year round. We made patties out of the new ones by scraping on a grater, squeezing the white milky starchy liquid out of them through a tea-towel, then shaping them into patties, and then frying them. We spread golden syrup over them – yum. They are called *pakeke*, and they have no other ingredients. It's no wonder I grew into a buxom lass. I can still hear him saying, "Eat up all your food, I'd rather have a tucker bill than a Doctor's bill". That was his way of nurturing.

When I see the words 'golden syrup' it reminds me of the molasses Father gave to his race horses. He really pampered his animals. I was taught how to groom them. I knew all about their hooves, fetlocks, the tuft at the back of the fetlock, and how to comb the mane. I knew the difference between a colt, a bay, a filly, pony, pie bald, gelding, stallion and others because he was always talking about them.

While I go on about Father and his brood, he also had other attributes. After all, he went to the Chathams as a school teacher (although I don't know whether he was registered or not) in Kaingaroa to begin with. That was how he met his wife-to-be. Our *whanau* lived at a place near Kaingaroa called Wairua. He told me the story about how he saw this beautiful woman with pretty eyes. He had his eyes set on her before she even guessed that he was trying to woo her. It is a beautiful love-story; it is a story I will savour all my life. Their love was never-ending, and he still spoke of her for years after she passed on, as if she was still in the room with us. I feel lucky to have had all those pensive moments with him. He obviously felt solitude in reminiscing like I do.

During the War while we were living in our old place at the beginning of the top road in Owenga, we sometimes stood on the front doorstep and when the wind was right we could see the shape of the trees across the bay towards Kaingaroa. Father pointed out all the landmarks and would say, "See, that's Te Whakaru where our Ancestors lived." Well being young and not really interested, I didn't concentrate, and I'm sorry now. If I was more attentive and more mature at the time, I could have gleaned so much history and *whakapapa*. It often sounded like a lesson. However, it is uncanny as I can still remember certain things, and hear his voice, but most times it's muffled. Little messages pop up now and then. Yet I suppose I deserve not being able to decipher his words because of my lack of interest at that time.

Another matter of interest, as a young man in Christchurch, Father also mastered the art of Tailoring. His work was so renowned that he was often in demand by the ladies of society to sew their finery. He also made men's suits. When hand sewing, he always waxed his cotton before threading the needle to give the thread strength and durability. The ball of wax was an amber colour which looked like toffee. We kids were tempted to bite it.

When Eileen went to Christchurch to work, it left Father and me on our own until Uncle Bunty retuned from World War II. Often family members stayed over with us. I can't ever remember him calling me by my name; it was always "my baby". The kids at school teased me for being such a big baby, and people often referred to me as 'that spoilt brat'. I guess he was a little over-protective. But on the other hand, there were times when he'd get really angry! I daren't mention all the flowery adjectives he used. He was known for using a flurry of blasphemous describing words. It was habitual with him to express himself in this verbal way. He often threatened to thrash Charlie and me, but we knew it was a whole lot of 'hot air' as he wouldn't harm a flea.

Father used to sew me singlets made out of winceyette to keep me warm – so he thought. I must say they were very well made, but they made me itchy, so I would sneak behind the gorse-bush on my way to school, take it off and hide it there, then forget to pick it up on the way home. One day on my arrival back from school he said, "Have you got your chemise on?" (pronounced shimmy). I quickly went into my room pretending I didn't hear him. When I thought he would have forgotten by now what he had asked me earlier, I went out. There he was with my chemise hanging on the end of his walking stick. "What is this?" he asked. Well, did I get the works. I was read the riot act in no uncertain terms. I was "encouraging ill health" and could end up with galloping consumption [TB] and goodness only knows what else, according to him.

Luckily his bark was worse than his bite. His language was blasphemous!! It would have frightened the living daylights out of any other kid. You mark my word, "You're never going to get another brass razoo out of me!" he would say. I realize now how adamant he was in trying to keep me 'a well child' and he cared so much for me that he wouldn't have been able to bare it if I did get sick. It was all merely 'hot air' threats as per usual.

Another time he found out that I had been smoking down in the sand-grass with friends. This time he made me stand up on the front doorstep and smoke his pipe and swallow until I became so dizzy that I felt like dying. He wouldn't let me stop until I was green and vomiting all over the step. That fixed my desire for dabbling in this smoking business for several years.

To punish me for doing something naughty, I would have to sieve the chaff, wheat and oats in readiness for feeding the race horses — a job I loathed. However, it was better than having to wipe all the leather harness with mutton bird oil. He fervently believed in this oil. He also rubbed his boots with it and anything else that needed oiling. A big advantage about this oil was that it was odourless. I'm talking about unsalted mutton birds, by the way. To savour the oil we roasted them on a cake rack over the top of a deep dish. This way you ended up with clean oil. This oil was great for frying bread and doughnuts. I had been in Nuhaka for years before I could eat a salted bird, as there is nothing like the fresh ones. Paraoa prae (friend scones) are beautiful cooked in this *titi* oil.

You would have thought that the 'eighth wonder of the world' had occurred when Lily was born (Uncle Bunty and Aunty Myrtle's first born of their seven children). It seemed like Father had also been 'born again'. He was 'over the moon'. Our baby only had to cough and he was away strutting down to the nursery — the sun porch attached to the main bedroom. It didn't matter to him if anyone thought he was interfering; he was smitten with this beautiful black-eyed dark-haired baby girl. And of course, with her being named after his wife, it was also special for him. It was so lovely to see just how much he loved us, and it was unconditional love.

I think I'm correct in saying that he was the culprit for the three broken bassinets. He rocked the 'billy-oh' out of them. He had a repertoire of songs that he sang over and over to Lily while rocking that cradle. It's a wonder she didn't start singing before talking. Believe me, they are still embedded in my head, and I'm sure they must be resonant in Lily's as well.

Being his first two grandchildren, Charlie and I were treated like precious china too, but as we grew older and became a little defiant he would get rather agitated and call us "insolent and impudent rascals" with a gust of adjectives from his other vocabulary. However, he still showered us with love, and I believe that love and nourishment are all that a child needs, and we certainly got that from him.

Aunty Myrtle and my brothers at the Air Base, about 1951.

Being Children

Back then life was continuously busy just trying to survive. Even though I was 'spoilt' by Father, I still had to do my share of the chores. But I am thankful for having to work because it has held me in good stead throughout my life. There was nothing much that I couldn't turn my hand to when it came to life skills. I knew how to head and gut a fish, cut the head off a chook, cut up meat, pluck birds, gather seafood, and a lot of other mundane every day jobs. I guess that's why I am a stickler for the old aphorism, "Don't talk if you can't walk the talk." Reminds me also of our SJC motto, "*I o mahi katoa mahia*" meaning "Whatever you do, do it well."

Life was so different as far as entertainment for children was concerned. We definitely had to make our own fun. We spent lots of time on the beaches, in fact we grew-up with sand between our toes and *raupa* (cracked skin) on our feet; *aue te mamae* (oh, the pain!). If we played in the pools the black peaty dirt was hard to get out of the cracks on our feet.

We roamed everywhere throughout our village. In fact we knew every nook and cranny, every cave and creek and crevasse. We were unified to our *whenua* and our *moana*. This was a pivotal part of our psyche. We wandered freely. We had complete freedom and ownership of 'our place'. We were the *tangata whenua / kaitiaki* (the people of the land) of Owenga. We grew up just like the wild flowers that grew out of the *whenua*; this is what makes us unique. There was no demarcation in our community or anywhere else on the Island for that matter. Yes, we were free as birds and as happy as sandlarks. Mainland New Zealand was 'over there somewhere'. We were fearful of nothing except the wild cattle and the odd big spiders which lurked amongst the trees in most areas. I certainly knew where to watch out for these critters as I was deadly scared of them. I might add that I am no better today. I could not hold one (no matter what size) if I was paid to. In fact I have made my grandchildren scared of them as well because of my reaction when I see one, even if it's small. Unfortunately, it's a phobia. There were always cob-webs strung across from branch to branch in our orchards and gardens. I was always aware so as not to run into one. Imagine the webs with a huge spider sitting in the middle waiting with baited breath for its prey. Been there and seen that — gives me goose-bumps just writing about them!!

When I was about seven years old I was frightened with a 'monster' of a spider from Southeast Island [an uninhabited Island lying a short distance out from Pitt Island]. One of the Donaldson Boys brought some back in a glass jar. They had been there to help with the shearing of some sheep. I think they supervised the running of the diesel generator. After the launch trip back to Owenga, these spiders were quite lethargic. He told me he had something for me and to close my eyes and hold my hand out. He gently put this monster of a spider in my hand. It covered my whole palm as it slowly spread out its legs!! I screamed and I think I fainted. My heart missed a few beats and I simply froze. What a "dumb" thing to do to an innocent kid. I had nightmares for years about spiders after that episode. From then on I always gave that chap a wide birth.

We girls often 'played' playhouses down in the small harbour where lots of coloured glass washed up on the beach. This was probably from the whaling days. These pieces had been well tossed and tumbled for years making them shapely and smooth.

Cousins Lily and Lou Preece, Uncle Bunty's daughters, early 1960s.

The brown pieces looked like toffee. We made shelves in our houses and lined them with this glass imagining they were our plates. Sandcastles were pretty decorated with this glass plus the shells from the beach. Lots of fanshells were around those days. Often when the men in the factory were gutting blue cod they would come across rows of bright fanshells in the gut. Apparently they swallowed these for ballast prior to a rough sea, so we had those to enhance our houses with as well. The 'wonder of nature' ... Imagine fish knowing that rough seas were coming. Every living creature must have a 'brain'.

My favourite playhouse belonged to my friend Ida. She had a flash one inside the Elderberry hedge at their place. Better still she had a lovely china tea set and other little pots and pans. We enjoyed many a cup of 'imaginary' tea. Best of all, her Mother made the nicest wee cookies, a child's delight. Her Mother was the best cook and baker. She baked every other day for the family. They had several boys in the family, and I think I can say without a doubt, they were the best fed men in Owenga. Murial was her name and she devoted all her time to cooking for 'the boys' and washing. They were her brothers.

She was well known for being a top cook. Everyone appreciated 'a cuppa' at Murial's place.

When I was about seven, I got from Santa (yes, we really did believe in Santa those days) a lovely little doll, a small wooden wash tub or bath and a small cake of soap. I also received in my parcel a bottle of 'hair oil'. These were exactly the things I had written to Santa for. How could I not believe in him. Hair oil was all the go those days. The boys used Bryill crème and the girls had hair oil. I wore my hair in long plaits, but in ringlets for church on Sundays, and plastered with hair oil on Saturdays, and nowhere to go!

We seldom got new clothes, like dresses and things. I think I got a new dress at Christmas time. I wore a dreaded gym-frock to school, and that was a bore and a chore. I only had two white blouses and had to wash them continuously. When I was old enough to ride to town, Father gave me extra money to buy me sandals and oddments. My very first purchase was always this bar of 'thick' chocolate ... remember, we didn't have a corner dairy in Owenga. Our parents had a mail order system, or catalogue buying set up with well known shops in Christchurch, and our basic clothes came that way. I'm sure most of our stuff came from Glasson's. That place has been in production for many years. The factory/warehouse was in Christchurch then and probably still is today.

However, Christmas wasn't only about Santa and gifts. It was also a time of worship. Our Nans as well as others in Owenga went to church on Christmas morning or sometime around about then. All depended on the Minister and the Priest because they had to come on horse-back from Waitangi. We always looked forward to Christmas dinner. We weren't interested in the roast lamb, home-made mint sauce, and fresh peas from our garden, plus all the other fresh veggies, or the *haangi* (food cooded in an earth oven). No, no, we were more interested in the 'Xmas Plum Duff.'

Outside our church, circa 1948. I have on a white hat, second from left in back.

We weren't too keen on the pudding itself; it was the thrupences and sixpences that attracted us kids. Oodles of small coins were mixed into this pudding. I have no idea what this signified, although this may have had something to do with the valuable gifts of frankincense and myrrh – gifts that were given to the Baby Jesus at his birth. The more we ate of it, the more money we were likely to find. This was cooked in real Plum Duff style – in a flour bag. We didn't have much room for anything else immediately after this. To penalize us for not eating our dinner first, we weren't allowed any trifle and jelly, even though it was Christmas. However, as the evening drew near, we were able to eat whatever we liked from the table. The table stayed set all day.

We often went on a picnic on Boxing Day and took all the leftover food. We sure appreciated that. Sometimes they would have a Gymkhana (horse sports) at the Owenga Station and that was fun. Everybody went to anything that was happening in the village.

As I mentioned earlier, Cousin Charlie and I often biked from Owenga to Whangamarino, in close proximity to Waitangi, some Fridays after school. Our job on Saturday was to cut gorse. Oh the pain! And the blisters ... and with Aunty Cissie setting the pace – wow what a task-master. We soon learnt what 'hard yacker' was. Sometimes we'd have to pluck the wool off the dead sheep. We were only kids doing a man's job. Our payment was a ticket to the flicks (movies) at the Waitangi Hall, which back then was down about where the Waitangi Fish Factory is today. Next door was the Post Office and Court House that were very close to each other and close to the beach. I had already left the Island when they moved all the buildings up to where they are today.

The very first film I saw was "Zoro Rides Again". I recall that the raspberry soft-drink in the glass bottle was just as exciting as the film. It was the first time I had seen a drink like that in a bottle — that colour anyway. We never had a shop in Owenga at that time.

During my last year at Owenga School we went to play sports at Te One School. The sports venue was in the paddock next to the Anglican Vicarage. The paddock was tidy and mowed. The most exciting part of the day for us Owenga kids besides winning some of the events [we were always lucky to have young Charlie and the fast-running Pomare whanau] was our short period of 'time-out' that was spent in Joe Wyeths shop. Oh it was like wonderland. It was next door to the school.

We stood and just gazed at the boiled lollies of many colours inside these big glass jars with fancy glass lids — a lure for any child, especially us Owenga natives. They were so shrewdly displayed slap bang in the middle of the counter, enough to make any child salivate.

During that same year I made a few trips to Waitangi on horseback to Grandma and Grand-dad Hough's place. I had no one to bike to Waitangi with now, as Charlie and his parents had gone to Pitt Island to work there for a time. These two lovely Nans were Aunty Myrtle's parents. While there I often made trips back to Joe Wyeth's shop. There were actually two rooms he used for shops, one on either side of the passage. He had groceries and those lollies on one side and all sorts of merchandise, clothing of every kind, as well as materials, cottons and haberdashery on the other side.

Clifford and Rhona also stayed with Grandma and Granddad. We often went mushrooming up in the back paddocks. The Sunday Hough family stayed up there. Mushrooms grew in abundance all around them. Grandma was a beautiful cook and when she dealt to them they were fit for a King to eat.

Also living up in this paddock was the old man Jacobs. He seemed very ancient to us. He was also a hermit, but one day he offered us some dried figs. We didn't really know what they were, but we ate them all the same. The after-effects had quite vigorous results, as one would imagine. We all raced home to the you-know-what. Everyone had outside 'dunnies' those days. We didn't have real toilet paper – we used news paper and sometimes brown paper. Only the government buildings had water toilets, they were sometimes called 'lavatories'. What a lonely existence this old man must have had, but in the end I think he looked forward to seeing us.

When I ponder over my childhood I realize that we were on the go all the time. We had very few bought things to play with. We had several board games such as Ludo, Draughs, Snakes and Ladders, card games like Snap, Kung-Kan, the older ones played Five-Hundred and Euchre. My favourite game was 'Crib' that is a game using a pack of cards and a 'crib board.' The board had holes in it. It was great to help with mathematics as it involved a lot of counting, multiplication, etc. Small pegs came with the boards. Some of the boards were oblong shaped, some were shaped like a triangle, and we also made the block out of an oblong bar of soap, put holes in it and used matchsticks for the pegs. We all played 'Patience'.

Then there were hop-scotch and marbles and quoits. Hop-scotch was played on the concrete at school or on the hard sand. We used empty tobacco tins or shoe polish tins for a skittle (I don't know if that's the correct name). Then with the quoits, these were circles made out of hard rubber. The idea was to throw them over this prong-like gadget situated on the ground a few feet in front of you, and the person who got the most quoits onto this spike was the winner. Duck shooting season we played with the empty cartridge shells, we didn't have many though, because our men had to go to the lake for duck and swan shooting, and that was too far away for us to go.

After our jobs were completed on a weekend we spent the rest of our free time outside. There was no such thing as sitting around inside unless the elements prevented us from going outside. We never went roaming or exploring until all our chores were done. Some didn't have the same workload. I had real hard jobs, like cutting wood and kindling, then milking the cow, then separating the milk and washing the separator. This had to be done before going to school. After school there were spuds to dig out and other jobs. This was after Aunty Myrtle and Uncle Bunty went to work on Pitt Island. Father and I went to stay with my birth Mother and my siblings. We were immediately across the road from Nanny Ngaria and Pa Jack. This was the year before I came out to secondary school.

If the tide was low after school, I sometimes went to get seafood for dinner. This was when all the men were away fishing. I seemed to be working hard during this period, and that is when I vowed I'd never go back to that Island until I was my own boss, even though once I did leave, I would miss Father like missing a limb. I wonder how I fit so much childhood playtime into my busy life of chores. I think it must have been due to not having TV or even a decent radio. I also think it was due to our long twilights in the summer months especially. We played a lot after tea in the summer, because it didn't get dark until about 9:30pm.

Cousins Lily and Lou Preece, early 1960s.

Uncle Bunty [Officer Alfred Preece Senior] during WWII.

Communication

A favourite pastime was listening to the 'wireless' (radio) at night. It was only allowed to be turned on at night. One of our favourite programmes was Dad and Dave of Snake Gully, and the 'hit parade' or the request session. During the War, Father insisted on listening reverently to the World News on a nightly basis because Uncle Bunty was serving in the 28 Maori Battalion. This was an intense period, although I was still too young and naïve to really understand the impact this War was having on Father and the other adults of our family. Uncle Bunty rose to the rank of Commissioned Officer in charge of 16 platoon of the 28 Maori Battalion D Company.

The important aspect as far as keeping the wireless going was to keep the battery charged. To do this we had to take the battery to the windmill which was situated on a small rise in our paddock, and clip it to the charger. The windmill dealt to it then. When I did it I took the battery on the wheelbarrow, because they were as big, or some were bigger and heavier than a car battery. There was nothing quite like watching the wind-mill rotating at 180 revolutions a minute!! The world of electronics was nowhere insight. It was hard to imagine that motor cars would ever go faster than 20 kilometres an hour, and that planes would be flying in and out almost daily.

Quite often our wireless sets clapped-out, this was when we had to take them to Sis Wagstaffe, this elderly man down the road. He was renowned for being the 'fix it' man where wireless sets were concerned. Today they are called "Radio Technicians." He was very clever, he had all the tools of the trade as well as a very good eyesight, because he tinkered in this dimly lit dungeon of a room which seemed to be cluttered with apparatus pertaining to the trade, plus dozens of wireless sets here and there. I guess some were old, and others would have been for parts, and others going through the 'fixing' stage. One would consider themselves lucky to get just a glimpse into his *whare*. To us kids it seemed kind of spooky and mysterious, something like a scary movie. Sis was actually a hermit and he never ventured outside of his yard that we knew of. Mrs. Hill his neighbour did all of his business and supplied him with his evening meal. One day I went across the paddock with my friend Joan Hill to take his meal. Although I had been there earlier on to take a wireless set for him to look at, I was by myself and felt a little scared to look around. This time going with my friend I thought I may be able to have a better look. I was quite excited at the thought of being able to have a peep. Seeing this little wizened-up old man who was peeping with beady eyes over the top of his glasses was quite bewildering. What made it scarier is that he didn't seem to like children. In fact I don't know who he liked.

Oddly enough, in spite of him being a recluse, he had the most delightful gardens — mainly flowers. The many colours of lupins and sweet-williams were a delight to the eye. I have never seen flowers like these since. Maybe he worked in his garden at night, early in the mornings or while we were at school. He had a hedge around his house so we would not have seen him anyway. Whatever he did it must have been the right thing. However, without him we would have been without wireless sets eventually.

Living across the paddock immediately next-door to the Hill family was another hermit by the name of Tom Suvich. He was Croation. Tom was a fisherman who lived in Kaingaroa before coming to Owenga. He lived in the paddock between Sis Wagstaff and the Hill family. His gardens were also a delight to the eye, again with a myriad of colours. I was fascinated with the brick path winding from the front gate to the front door of his house. We sneaked down there sometimes just to stand at the gate and gaze at the 'fairytale' gardens. Whenever I'm in a pensive mood I often lapse into reminiscent mode and my thoughts wonder back to that scene that instantly evokes my memory — a perfect natural display that tickled my fancy, and is still a vivid picture in my mind today. We always thought these two men were in competition with each other in a quiet unassuming way. Tom also had a hedge around his house. That is why those two old 'Codgers' had such great success with their gardens.

After the War ended, telephone communication began. I can't remember just how many phones were installed; all I know was that it seemed like magic to me and most of the other kids in Owenga. Of course we were all on a party line. That created a few commotions; I decline to say 'how'! The manual board was operated from the Telephone Exchange in Waitangi. Later a more robust Radio Link was set up between Pitt Island and the Chathams. This was such an asset for our Pitt Island *whanau*. When I say there were moments, I have to say just how much fun Charlie and I had 'listening in'. We had no idea that others on the line knew who we were. Yes, it was fun until this voice said, "Put that phone back, Val." Well, I think I fell off the stool with fright. I was almost scared of it after that. We were so ignorant about telecommunication, but that's how it was back then. We soon learnt.

Wash Days

On Saturdays there was the large load of washing to be done. I was going onto 13 years old at the time, and working like an adult. First of all, the copper had to be lit. The sheets plus the other whites were boiled in the copper. We slept with one white sheet on top of us and a grey blanket on the bottom in place of an under sheet. There were about nine children at the time.

We used a substance called "Ricketts Blue" that acted as a whitening agent. This block of blue solid pumice looking stuff was sealed in a little cotton bag about the size of a cotton reel. This was swished around in the rinsing water until it became light blue in colour, then the whites were rinsed. It was important to use this blue sparingly, because if too much was used, the clothes were inclined to go too blue instead of white. One block lasted for several washes. Things seemed to last a lot longer then, fortunately. This was a great invention, but it went off the market about fifty-something years ago.

There were no washing machines in those days. Every washhouse had a washboard, and these were either made of glass or wood. They had a sort of corrugated surface that you rubbed the clothes up and down on. You rubbed the clothes with soap first. This friction seemed to get the dirt or grime out of the heavy garments. This method saved our hands. We used our home-made soap for rubbing the clothes with, and Rinso Powder in the copper when boiling.

I would work my way through the pile of washing that took all day to do. I hung the sheets and towels on the line, and when I ran out of space, I hung the next lot on the fence, then the last load went on the fence across the road. Luckily we lived down the end of Owenga and our washing wasn't in view of the public, not that it really mattered. The other big *whanau* were the Pomares who also had big wash days. Then Muriel Donaldson must have washed daily, because they had a big family of boys. She always had white linen and towels fluttering on the line. Her boys were engineers and they had a garage where they did repairs. I think she must have washed their gear regularly, as they never looked 'greasy' at all. Most times there was plenty of wind to dry the clothes. Just about every day was a good day for washing.

To make soap, the main ingredient we used was mutton fat, then caustic soda and resin. We would pour in water and bring to boil, then simmer; add baking soda and borax. When the mixture is off the boil, you can add one teaspoon of citronella to make it smell nice, or any other scent from a chemist. I can't remember the measurements of the ingredients. We poured our mixture into a tin (a kerosene tin cut length-wise) and let it set. When hard it was cut into bars, and it was always a satisfying feeling to stand back and admire our soap. We often ran out of imported washing soap and every day necessities because of irregular shipping.

While I'm on the subject of soap, there was another soap we used often and called 'sand-soap'. This was a big block of grey soap similar to solvol soap in colour. We scrubbed our big wooden dining table with it, as well as the back door step. It was used mainly for unvarnished wood and to get black off pots after cooking over a flame.

All these important life skills are what I'd like to pass onto my *mokopuna*. Judging by the way the world is looking today, I think that we may need to revert back to the basics someday. When I voice my concerns to my grand daughters, they laugh and say, "Oh, Nan!" I'm sure they think I'm from another planet! They don't know what I mean when I say, "Use your imagination when you have leftover food." If it's still edible, it can be turned into another delicious dish – 'shepherds pie' is one example, when there is leftover cold meat or mince. But I suppose that's the sign of the times, and perhaps I'm simply 'old fashioned'.

On a much lighter note, we actually did get up to mischief at times. I'd like to think of it as a healthy outlet for us kids and all part of growing up. I realize now that we had other things that compensated for the lack of every day commodities. We had rock-pools, white beaches, our cave that we had so much fun in, and all the different 'posies' for certain shells. Then there was a variety of fish in the mouth of our biggest creek; that gave us a lot of pleasure. We really had healthy surroundings. There were so many nooks and crannies that belonged to "us" and probably haven't been discovered and explored yet by the most recent residents.

Next to Manukau is "the brook" which I have mentioned earlier. Sometimes during summer we took our washing there on a sledge pulled by bullocks. There was a freshwater well there, and believe it or not, we really did run out of water during a dry summer.

Our Hawaiki creek, our lagoon, the lakes and Te Awa *inanga* are all 'living organisms'. They have a life force that provided the source of sustainability for everyone. These are precious resources, and in those days with irregular shipping, we were even more reliant on our natural resources.

Home Remedies

During the War we had malted milk at school during morning interval. Immediately after our fingernail and handkerchief inspection, the copper was lit to boil the water; the seniors had turns doing this. We used a gadget with several holes in it, something like a huge potato masher that we pumped up and down in this vat after we had added the milk powder, cocoa and boiling water. This resulted into the most tasty and frothy chocolate malted milk. Who said we didn't know about 'chocolate lattes' those days. All the children lined up with their own personal mugs.

Much to our dislike, (just to spoil it all) we also had to have a teaspoon of cod liver oil at morning interval. But then after that, at lunch time we were issued with an apple. These apples were red delicious and the smell was tantalizing. The older folk will remember the apples being wrapped individually in tissue then packed into a wooden apple box.

I think we were given this fruit because of the War. The exporters were unable to ship them out of the country at times, so most schools in NZ enjoyed this fruit. In fact the schools in the mainland also had a bottle of milk at playtime. This issuing of milk lasted for quite sometime after the War.

We must have been lucky to have a boat come at the right time. The mind boggles – what has gone wrong with our country, when you take into account the price of milk today!!

Well, if the cod liver oil and an 'apple a day' wasn't enough to keep the Doctor away, Father insisted I have a dessert-spoon of this horrible cough mixture called "Lanes Emulsion." It was just as vile as the cod liver oil. This was a ritual every night. Nevertheless, I really can't remember ever having the flu as a child. I realize now that was pretty incredible for having grown up in such a damp environment, and we played a lot in ponds, sea and creeks.

Another important health factor was that the Nannies had their own remedies, whether it be common medication sold over the counter or by using their own native medicinal flora and fauna. Living on a remote island (that was far more remote those days), one needed to adhere to the advice of the Elders. I still take heed of some *rongoa* (native plant medicine) from what I learnt when growing up on our Motu o Rekohu / Wharekauri (Chatham Islands).

During my early adult life I thought about the fresh vegetables, berries, seafood, wild foods like *puha* (similar to dandelion), watercress, and the birds like wild duck, swan and *weka* that we ate, and I realized that very few of us had ever been sick. All our food was absolutely organic. We feasted on wild berries, sweet potatoes (these were the ones left in the ground after harvesting) the wild peas were similar to the mung beans we buy today at a exorbitant price, the taste was the same. We sucked the nectar from the *korari* (flax flower) during the spring when they were fat and lush. *Harakeke* grows prolifically on the Island, and it's found in most places. I think it was used a lot for shelter belts. I had never been to a Doctor or in a hospital as a patient until going into the maternity annex to have my first baby.

During the spring time at school, when the playtime bell rang, we all made for the succulent Korari to suck on the nectar. Shame on us, as this was the domain of the Tui (native songbird). On seeing us coming, they would just casually flutter in such a docile manner over to the outer bushes, beyond our reach, and slowly returned when we went away. They were never scared of us. It wasn't until years later that I read that the Tui become quite inebriated on the nectar of the *korari*, hence the reason for them being in sort of a 'drunken coma'. The wonder of nature never fails to amaze me.

Yes, we ate the red berries off the box-thorn bushes, and sucked the fluffy purple inner of a certain thistle plant that grew near our beloved Hawaiki creek. I never saw one anywhere else on the Island. It may have been a survivor of the Prendeville gardens. We also enjoyed the edible *poroporo* (nightshade) berries. These were ripe during the main potato-picking season.

I can't recall seeing more than one frost during my time. It has been said that it's because the Island is so low lying and the sea envelopes our villages. In fact a frost was such a rare sight that I didn't really know what it was when I came upon this pond on my way to school with a glassy looking glaze over it. We couldn't help but play with it, and even had a try of sucking it!! How gross when I think of it now. I never saw snow either until I came to Napier. But, as we have all come to realize, Mother Nature works in mysterious ways, thus anything goes now as far as the weather is concerned. I heard that there were hailstones as big as gooseberries on the Island in 2010.

Back then the climate was great for growing anything as long as there was shelter. I have seen potatoes growing all year round, probably due to the lack of frosts. I can't ever remember having to buy spuds. Our favourite potato was a Maori *taewa* (now known as a heritage potato) called *nga-aute-aute*. Some people called it *natooti* or *ngatioti*. The senior Islanders will know what I mean. All breeds grew prolifically and still do today. When we had no plugs for our sinks (until the next boat), we made one by peeling a raw potato and shaping it to the size of the plug. This served the purpose perfectly.

The Chatham Islands used to be well-known for their potato cropping for export. From 1845-1856, about 7,000 tonnes of potatoes were exported from the Island. About the same time, 3,950 bushels of wheat were also exported. Several Australian trading vessels regularly stopped at the Chathams. Imagine what one could produce today with all the more modern implements. The soil must be screaming out to be tilled in some places.

When I think of the remedies and cures used in those days, it really becomes a trip down memory lane. Some may poo-hoo it these days, but I can't help but wonder if we may have to revert to the old ways someday when I look at the mess New Zealand is in today, and the economic situation at the moment. 'Kiwi ingenuity' may have to be exercised more often.

We chewed on *koromiko* (a type of *hebe*) for stomach ailments, especially diarrhoea. Bruised leaves were heated and used as a poultice for ulcers and boils. Sometimes we mixed baking soda with a drop of water into a *koromiko* paste to ease the itch and get rid of the bight mark from certain insects by just rubbing over the infected area.

We also ate the *kopi* berries after they had been cooked. You can eat the soft golden skin off this berry once it is ripe, but definitely not the kernel until they are cooked. This is an art, as you need to rid them of toxins. Most people liked these berries. I like them better than peanuts, and I still cook them today. We have trees here but I never collect them from just anywhere – I need to know the *whakapapa* of the tree. In the olden days our *whanau* buried their babies' afterbirths underneath these trees. Any human remains that are buried make the area *tapu* (sacred), thus it becomes *wahitapu* (sacred ground). One needs to respect all of that.

We found the plant *kawakawa* useful for many ailments, and even ordinary bread was used for poultices that was applied hot to a sore, like a boil, to draw out the core. As well as bread poultices, we also mixed a concoction of bar soap and sugar. This was then applied to the affected area. Sometimes we drank water in which gorse flowers had been boiled. Another thing about gorse — I recall the Elders saying, "When the gorse is in full bloom, the *kina* is fat and sweet." The old folk also maintained that "When the white *manuka* is in full bloom, the *kina* is at its fattest." I believe so, as I have witnessed this.

We ate the berries off the *kawakawa* bush; they were lovely when they were yellow. Kawakawa grows abundantly, and it is

Kawakawa leaves and berries.

renowned to cure many ailments such as boils, kidney problems, and to relieve the pain of a toothache (by chewing the leaves). As a blood purifyer, we infuse the leaves in boiling water (like when making tea), then drink it.

About 30 years ago I bought a tree from our local nursery. I cook the berries off that tree. Then about 25 years ago, one of my daughters brought one berry back from the Owenga Station, put it in a pot and sort of forgot about it. Well, it grew like a mushroom. It is now flourishing in my backyard, and every year dozens of young ones appear. I will end up with my own *kopi* grove or a canopy of *kopi*. Another quality they have is that they are evergreen.

Then to get rid of chewing-gum on clothing, we would rub it with oil of eucalyptus, then wash in hot soapy water. For earaches, we would heat a whole onion in the oven, then place it in a clean sock and hold to the ear as long as possible. Bathing with Epsom salts in the water eased aches and pains. For bee stings, we spread honey over the stung area. To purify the blood, we dissolved a desert-spoon of molasses in a cup of warm water, then drank it. Father also drank krusion salts dissolved in a glass of warm water — he drank this almost daily. For a sore throat, he would skin an onion and slice finely, sprinkle with brown sugar, leave overnight, then drink the liquid the next morning. When we ran out of toothpaste, we used ashes on our toothbrushes. Our bought toothpaste was a pinky colour that came in hard, flat small tins. Sometimes we used salt as well.

Kopakopa is another common medicinal weed used to draw puss out of sores. Just squash the leaves and place on an effected area, then tightly bandage. Don't leave on too long though.

These are just a few of the handy hints that come to mind at the moment. Mind you, I have applied some of them to my own *mokopuna* over time, and I must add, it has been beneficial. Some of these hints are worth bottling.

Speaking of bottling reminds me of the homemade brew Father made. I'd give anything for a swig of that brew today, the 'nectar of the gods.' This was made in a big wooden barrel. The only ingredients I remember are the sultanas, malt, sugar and hops. The aroma of the fermentation of the hops sure activated the thirst-buds. It seemed like 'forever' waiting for it to infuse into a brew. My job was to stir it often. You had to wait for the raw potato to float to the top, and then it was ready for consumption. This beverage was consumed by the grown ups mainly when they were around the card table. Amusing how the laughter got louder and the thumping of the cards also became more audible after a few glasses of these fermented hops. I guess they too had to make their own fun. These are such lovely memories.

Trading and Shops

I remember having to go along to Shelly Beach driving the sledge to get a sack of grit for our chooks. Previously a gentleman manufactured this grit along there, and I believe he had a great export trade operating. He had long gone by the time I was old enough to drive along there. There were still fragments of the shell-crushing trade. The evidence was also visible in the bags of grit that were left stacked inside this derelict building. This house was almost on the beach, and for years after, only the chimney stood forlorn on the fore-shore. I remember seeing it on visits back home. He would have had ample shell to work with because this particular beach has an abundance of all kinds of shell probably one foot deep on the beach, hence the name I guess. There must be heaps of shellfish out from there and maybe a reef because the sea doesn't come up over that spot unless perhaps with a freak tide. A reef would break the force of the waves and is most likely to be the breeding ground for all that shellfood.

While writing about this area another vivid memory comes to mind — the big black rocks that lie below where this house was situated. Some of us went along there to gather these huge *kuku* (mussel) shells for the Nans to scrape their *harakeke* (flax) with when they were making the *'muka'* (flax fibres) for the handles of their *kete* (kit or basket). I have seen those huge mussels but we couldn't 'take to them' — we preferred eating the smaller type called *'taere'* which are found on the rocks below Te One creek and at the cattle yards below the Owenga Station. These were our favourites. In season when they are fat, they are very succulent. During my trips back to the Island I intended going along to those black rocks, but some how I never got to see those big *kuku* mussels again.

When thinking about a Hindu man who had a grit business, I remember this shop that was situated diagonally down from the Owenga church, St. Barnabas. This corrugated iron shop sat a few metres up from the Hawaiki creek on the side of the bank along side of the track going over the hill to the main harbour. I believe this gentleman was trading around 1926-1945. I vaguely remember him and his shop. He was the same Mr. Dinn who set up shop in Waitangi. He no doubt saw that the grass was greener on the other side, as the Fishing Industry was on a wane and most of the fisher people had moved from Owenga to greener pastures as well. The shop he had in Waitangi was down on the corner not too far away from where the Works Infrastructure workshop is today. By the time I was able to ride to town I often went there to gaze at the sparkling rings he had on display in this glass cabinet, dreaming of owning one myself 'when I grew up'. I realized later that all that glitter is not gold. Apparently he was an old 'rogue'.

There was another shop-come-post-shop further up the Hawaiki creek across the main road in Owenga. This was owned by Mr. Earnest Guest. He started his business around 1927. He didn't trade for too long owing to the economic situation at that time. He must have carried some valuable merchandise, as kids we used to fossick in the remains of what must have been a lovely house. One day we stumbled over several valuable pieces. My prize 'find' was a pair of brass candle-sticks. They became a very useful item, as every house-hold used candles those days. It's amazing how we never had accidents with candles while

Bridge over Te Awa Inanga.

waltzing around with them throughout the house. This was probably because we were never allowed to carry a lit one without a candle-stick, even a jam jar sufficed. There were all sorts of shapes and sizes of these sticks. Some were very ornate, some made of glass, china, enamel and even crystal. They would be a collectors delight today. The coloured glass vases and ornaments were also beautiful. We found many lovely items under the growth of old gardens. I have wondered since whether he may have buried these things for safe keeping and later forgotten where he hid them.

Although Mr. Guest closed shop earlier than he anticipated he stayed on living in Owenga. There is a place at the back of Owenga Station named after him, I think it might be "Guests Camp". He must have grown a flourishing garden of vegetables and flowers and shrubs, because the remnants were still there when we were kids. That was where I saw my first red flowering *manuka* — it was so pretty.

Shearing competition on the Island, circa 1950s-1960s.

Kai, Kai, and More Kai

I seem to be always writing about what we ate as if that was all we did. Believe me, there was much more to life than that. We worked hard, as I have already said, and we never had a shop or dairy just around the corner. I now realize that the reason we kids were always sucking nectar from plants and eating every edible berry was probably because we were deprived of sweets like the mainland kids enjoyed, and our bodies might have been lacking in certain carbohydrates. However, I must add that we did have a visit from a dentist annually, and I can't remember any of us kids ever having to have fillings or any such scary work done. So perhaps being deprived was really of benefit to us in a way.

We lived off the Island resources, and these had to be grown, hunted, harvested and prepared. Our meat, fish, and vegetables were fresh. We did have treats, but these were few and far between because of irregular shipping. I don't think there was a young person who wasn't au fait with the art of making toffee or fudge, but as you would imagine, one had to earn the privilege.

All our other goods were brought in on coastal trading ships. These boats only came three or four times a year. Flour came in 25lb. bags — four of these to a sack. These sacks were worth their weight in gold, as were the white flour bags. The sacks were so versatile. We used them for backdoor mats and *pikau* bags, or split-sacks. This *pikau* was flung over the back of a horse under the saddle; it had splits on both sides, acting as carry bags. These were handy to take to Lake Te Awa Patiki when the men went hunting, and swan-egging.

Sugar also came in a 25lb. bag. I'm sure everyone knows what a sugar bag looks like. These also had a multitude of uses. Elaborate oven cloths were made out of them, as well as aprons or 'pinnies' as we called them. We put our cooked *kopi* berries in them before steeping in a swift-running creek. They were ideal for this because of their durability.

Today I steep my berries in a plastic bucket, and change the water every day for about five days.

Aunty Myrtle got her honey in a 4 gallon tin, which was the same size as a kerosene tin. Imagine the cost of that amount of honey today. Then mixed nuts (still in their shells) were in sugar bags. This was bulk buying! The 4 gallon tins were also put to many uses. Cut in half diagonally, they served as an ideal dish for roasting swan and other big birds. Left whole, they were handy to cook crayfish in. And the kerosene tins were great to *tahu* (preserve) birds and meat in. This is a method when the food is cooked and set in its own fat.

Then there were the 7lb. tins of golden syrup. When empty we put a wire handle on them and used them as 'billies'. They were like small pails, thus very handy to take to the freezers to carry cod livers and roes in. We also used them during blackberry picking season. We carried all sorts of things in these after they were converted into buckets. Very little was discarded those days – we utilized everything. This was survival and resilience.

I can still see the 24 gallon drum three quarters full of swan eggs in our pantry. Swans lay in spring around the edges of the lagoon. They also build nests and lay on small islands on the lake. The eggs were preserved by rubbing this Vaseline-looking substance called ovoline around them. This was real egg-preserving emollient. Needless to add, we had sufficient eggs to last until the following season, and most people had their own chooks, some even had geese. Eggs were handy to have and everyone baked their own cakes and biscuits. There were always functions, and because we weren't able to buy things suitable for an evening out, the women had to do their own baking for their 'plate'. Nobody went anywhere with 'nothing'. The women always took something and it was the same all over the Island. As a matter of interest, a swan egg is equivalent to five hen eggs.

All households had storerooms. The Harveys had a big one with shelves all around the walls. After the ship had arrived, these shelves were packed with approximately a six-months supply of non-perishable groceries. Everything came in bulk packaging. One item that stands out in my mind is the tobacco – about 24 inners to an outer (carton). There were several brands; Park Drive, Greys and Black and White. That is where I acquired the tobacco that Father had found out about, as mentioned earlier. I got up to tricks when I had to babysit. I often had to mind my younger siblings on Family Benefit days. All the Mothers in Owenga went to Waitangi for the day. My friend would come and visit me. One time I decided to open a packet of jelly called "Luscious". Inside the packet sitting on top of the crystals was this hard lolly-like looking thing wrapped in see-through paper. We had great delight in sucking these. We didn't realize that these jubes contained the 'setting fluid'. No need to add that there were a few frustrating moments when the jellies never set.

Making toffee was another skill we perfected. There was always plenty of sugar and homemade butter. The hardest part was trying to keep the fire stoked so as to allow the sweets to boil rapidly so to stop the sweets from going sugary and setting properly. The next hardest part was trying to devour the lot before anyone arrived home.

I think most of us knew from youngsters how to make bread and doughnuts (we called them floaters or fried bread). These were often made from the bread dough after it had risen. We also made them by mixing dough of flour, baking powder and milk or water. To make a change from kneading the dough into loaves and baking it, we'd shape it into doughnuts. The main thing when cooking them was to make sure the fat/dripping/oil was heated to the ideal temperature, as it had to be hot to prevent the bread from absorbing too much fat.

Another time Aunty Myrtle and Uncle Bunty went to Waitangi and stayed over night. I rang my friend to come and stay with Father and me. Part way through the day I remembered I had to let the chooks out and collect the eggs. There were eggs everywhere. I think we must have collected at least two dozen that day. When putting them into the container, they kept falling out onto the bench because there wasn't enough room in the bowl. Aah — we came up with a brainwave, we decided to make some sponges. I knew there was all this food colouring in the pantry, so we decided to make different coloured cakes. We didn't have an electric beater — we used hand-beaters those days. You can imagine all the beating. Father was quite confused and asked what we were doing. I replied that we were making 'a' cake. To cut a long story short, we ended up with a blue, red and green sponge. Not being able to do justice to them all, consequently some ended back in the chook house. We kept that secret for years.

About twenty years later, I told Aunty Myrtle about it, and she laughed and laughed. She said that she would had never guessed as there were so many eggs, sugar and flour in those big bags, it wasn't noticeable that we had used anything. I really don't believe she would have got angry if she did know. She was such a sweetie, and she treated me like her own. Father just adored her; she was so good to us. Whenever I had to do errands for her he insisted I jump to attention and do them immediately, and I did. I never had any qualms about doing something for Aunty Myrtle. Somehow I knew when not to err on the edge of caution. I can't ever remember having any bitter feelings towards her. I always *felt* the love she had for us, and the feeling was mutual; respect for one another was relevant.

Most of us had our own cow or cows and made our own butter, so there was no shortage of the basics. There was even cream on request. The folk in Waitangi and Te One were rather lucky because they had the cheese factory nearby. This cheese factory was situated in Te One. They exported the cheese, and I believe it was a top-notch product.

Another enjoyable venture was *weka* hunting on a moonlit night up at Patiki. Uncle Charlie had a 'cracker-jack' of a bird dog called Micky. He knew exactly where to grab the bird so as not to damage it. He brought the bird to you live. These dogs were trained to do this so you could kill the *weka* yourself by squeezing its heart, the heart being up near the neck. As I mentioned before, by killing it this way, the bird was tender. If the bird was too skinny you simply let it go. That was the whole idea of the dog bringing it to you live. That was our custom anyway.

There was an abundance of cockles, eels and flounders, and in season also swan, duck and *weka* up at Patiki. Patiki is situated on the southeast side of the lagoon near Owenga. There was watercress to cook with the *weka* as well, and also clumps of thyme, suitable for when stuffing and stewing the swan and ducks. I do believe that Nan [Lily] planted the thyme there. Now it's growing wild. Easter was a good time to go to the lake because the *weka* were fat at that time. Out of season they are skinny and inedible, mainly because they are laying and hatching.

Up inside the shelter of the sand dunes was an ideal place for setting up camp. There was plenty of wood because of the fallen *akeake* trees. This was always a touch of paradise for all of us. We made the best of our trips away from home. We played in the lake, we roamed and woved our way in and out of the vegetation and the bush-clad Point amongst the wild flora and fauna that created sponge-like cushioning under our feet. This was one of the most peaceful places for us, so much so that even at that age I could 'feel' the presence of our indigenous *Karapuna* (Ancestors), more so if this certain mist was enveloping us and the *patupaiarehe* (spiritual beings similar to fairies) were dancing with us. I will always yearn for even just a glimpse of that *wahi tapu* (sacred place) and to catch a whiff of our lake — Te Whanga Lagoon.

We always knew there must have been scallops out from the mouth of the Lagoon as there were always heaps of shells on the beach up in that area. Years later trawlers were dredging for this 'gold of the sea' up near Okawa, north of Owenga. Tonnes were fished out of there. The Fishers became millionaires overnight. Some clever fishers also owned crayfish and *paua* quota. The seabed was like an untouched gold mine.

I only hope that if all these fish, crayfish, oysters and scallops, ever do regenerate again to that degree, that the Islanders will manage their resources to their advantage. My heart sinks when I think of the millions of dollars that 'outside fishers' reaped from the Island during the Crayfish Boom — and left nothing! I haven't heard the Islanders themselves complaining about that crayfish rush when all those boats from the mainland rushed in and some were fouling up the grounds by 'heading at sea'. That is what's buggering-up the world today: greed. I remember reading in the papers at that time how the Chatham Islands were 'raped' by outside fishers, and I agree.

Hunting and preparing food *was my life*. It was the survival of the fittest, I suppose. We had no TV and we weren't allowed to listen to the wireless during the day, or sit around inside, so I preferred to be outside. We didn't have many books to read except for the reading we brought home from school. We were all of the same ilk on the Islands so the fundamental skills for preservation of food in such an environment was part of daily life; in fact, these tasks were mundane. Preserving meat and birds as well as fish was usually done by smoking or storing in fat. I was not keen on this *tahu* food when I was young, but if offered to me now I wouldn't hesitate. I have since acquired the taste. When I now think about the tahu mutton birds and other big birds and *'miti tahu'* my mouth waters.

We were lucky to have such an abundance of fresh natural foods, especially during the War years. During the War all families were issued with coupons. From memory I think they were like detachable tickets that one put over the counter when purchasing goods. In other words, people were rationed, perhaps the price and the amount of goods depended on the size of the families. I hope I haven't misled you too far away from the facts. The only knowledge I remember about these coupons is hearing the adults talking.

By the time I was ready for the big wide world, the cargo ships and flying-boats became more regular, and people started buying their butter, bread and other dry commodities.

I went at least once a week to the fish freezer to collect cod roes and livers and heads for us, and Nanny Ngaria and Pa Jack too. The livers and roes are delicious rolled in flour and fried in hot oil or drippings. I truly think that caviar takes second place to cod livers and roe. After all, caviar is also a fish (sturgeon) roe. Some people rave on about it, probably because it's so expensive and poshy. I see nothing in it myself, except that its priced beyond its worth.

We actually ate like Kings, although we sometimes felt hard-done-by. We had nothing, yet we had everything. It was so often quoted, "We had plenty of nothing." We would have appreciated some sausages. We were all in the same boat, yet I must add we were all so happy. We were like one big family in Owenga, and I'm sure it was the same elsewhere on the Island.

We were all united so much more as 'Islanders'. I guess because we probably all relied on one another in more ways than one.

Now they say milk is bad for some, plus eggs and butter and cheese — all the foods we were brought up on, *and* they cost a fortune. Today we are eating some foods that are full of imitation ingredients that make it last longer on the shelves ... how unnatural is that! You would be shocked if you investigated what goes into some margarines. Some even have plastic in them!! Sometimes I wonder if that is why we are being cursed with all these sicknesses such as diabetes, cancers, heart disease, high blood pressure, joint pains etc.

The world is full of greed and power seekers. The so-called food experts advise us to eat lots of fruit and vegetables, margarine and watered-down milk — just like the skimmed milk we gave to the pigs after separating it. One thing is for sure; we never had access to any of that food back in the Chathams. I can not reiterate enough just how organic we were, and yet we always felt a bit under-privileged for not being able to have processed modern foods.

During the bird-laying season, we rode up along Hanson Bay and up through "the cutting" (the opening in the sand dunes) and along the inside of the sand hills, in the bracken to look for noddie eggs. A noddie is a small sea and land bird similar to a seagull, but a lot smaller. We took our 'billies' and cooked our eggs there. Sometimes we would take bread and have a little picnic.

Recently I have eaten quails eggs. A friend of mine rears them for the market. The eggs are very much like the noddie ones, and they sell for more than $5.00 a dozen — quite expensive when that amount would fit easily into a small soup bowl. As a matter of interest, they are the image of a noddie egg to look at — the spots, size, shape and the taste. When they are prepared for the table, the quails themselves are very expensive to buy.

They are in great demand at the top restaurants. Who knows ... one could start up an interesting enterprise from inside those sand dunes!

On some weekends when Charlie and I went to Whangamarino and had a well-earned break from cutting gorse, we roamed around the back of the farm and around to Uncle Jack Kamo's place at Waikato. The blackberries and mushrooms were ready at the same time, and on one of our escapades the mushrooms were so plentiful that we were walking over them, and kicking the puffballs every where. We weren't able to take any home because Aunty Cissie couldn't stand the sight or the smell of them. We couldn't resist picking some blackberries as they were so plentiful and we didn't have many bushes in Owenga.

The Kamo house was situated on the hill above Lake Huro diagonally below where the Moriori Marae stands today. The two macrocarpa trees are still there and are visible from the Marae. That is where their freshly killed mutton hung to set.

Uncle Jack Kamo's house was over this hill next to Lake Huro, and the macrocarpa trees were where the mutton hung to set.

Lena Kamo was my friend. I would 'bully' Charlie to come across the paddocks with me so that I could see her. It was lovely meeting up with each other at one of our Chatham Island picnics in Napier. She was living in Wellington at that time. Unfortunately, she has since passed on — Bless her soul.

Sadly, we no longer have those get-togethers now since our Elder and Organizer Joe Tuanui passed on — Bless his soul too. That knowledgeable man knew 'all' the Chatham Island history and the *whakapapa* of most of the Islanders. He told us lots of stories at those meetings. I wish I had recorded them. His mind was like an encyclopaedia of the Chatham Islands and its people, and what matters more, he was a real 'true blue' person. He spoke only the truth, he never said anything just to please people, neither did he make things up. His word was *pono*, meaning absolutely true. He was a direct descendant of Ngahiwi Dix and had no reason to do any investigating to find out who he was. He simply knew the Dix *whakapapa* inside out. We all admired that man for his honesty and integrity, and he also walked the talk. It's a pity he isn't here today to put the Ngahiwi Dix whakapapa in its correct place for all of her descendants.

His widow Gwen also knows a lot of history. She often entertained us with her interesting stories about what life was like for her when she first arrived on the Island as a young bride from New Zealand. She told us about having to make bread using the sap from certain flax when they had run out of yeast. This sap acted like a rising agent. Joe's Nanny would give her instructions. Gwen had difficulty in understanding the old Lady because she spoke in pigin English being fluent in Maori — Ngati Mutunga dialect of course. It is interesting how she learnt survival skills from this old Woman, as Joe was (like his descendants today) busy out on the farm, forging a living for his family. Gwen and her daughter Janice now live in Hastings. She kindly lent me some photos.

For those of you who don't know the Chathams, the Tuanui family lived way up towards the northwest end of the Island up near Te Reto Paraoa, a long way (those days) from us in Owenga. I knew Jack Tuanui [Joe's brother] very well — he was a gentleman in every way, and a great Skipper and fisherman. This family really are the toilers of the land, and evidence is visible on the Island today.

Can you see all the paua exposed on the rocks?

The Weather

Some people may think I am being optimistic when I go on about the Island and its beauty, because not everyone who has been there is of the same opinion, and listening to the weather forecast is enough to put some people off going there. It must sound like the 'back end of hell' to some. But, let me reassure you it ain't all that bad.

Nevertheless, this is how I remember Chatham Island, and what makes it like this is the fact that I am affiliated to the place, I guess. The weather can 'pack-up' and the prevailing sou'westerly winds can blow like 'billy-oh' but it does the same here on the mainland in the winter. There the winds blow at such a velocity because of the low-lying physical character of the Island. By the same token I have to admit that I have felt sorry on some of my flights back home when there are complete strangers disembarking the plane in a howling sou'westerly. True, not everything is rosy, but inclement weather isn't always on the itinerary. The sun makes an appearance quite often in the summer months.

Because the soil in Owenga is so productive, all one needs to grow a garden is time and energy. Many a time I have heard people say, "You can't grow anything on the Chathams; it would become airborn with all the howling gales they have."

I get quite indignant, and I don't give much credence to that remark. Unfortunately, the weather on the forecast isn't always accurate. A lot of what is predicted on the forcast fizzes-out at sea before reaching the Chathams. But, again I can't pretend that the weather over there is all sunshine and blue skies either. The prevailing winds can be destructive and devastating. Some compare the Chatham Island climate as being similar to the Southern Wairarapa. Shelter belts are the answer, I always reiterate.

The weather on the Chathams can be so very unpredictable, you could sometimes experience four seasons in one day. It has been said because the Island is so low-lying with very few hills; this is one of the main reasons for these very varied weather conditions. There were times when the wind whipped-up suddenly without any warning, and Manukau Reef became a mountainous sea of frothy white caps. This situation really tested the durability and sturdiness of the little wooden launches and the capabilities of the skippers. There was no ship-to-shore communication; hard to comprehend in this day of modern technology and GPS. Imagine being cut off from the rest of the world.

When suitable, we would stand on the rise up on the road and watch for the boats as they ploughed through that reef, sometimes with our hearts in our mouths. We'd wait in anticipation for the first glimpse. Somehow we had a feeling when the boats were about to appear — some sort of telepathy. I still have those intuitions today. Some say it's a gift, and I guess it is, but it can also be very spooky, especially when some of the visions are quite foreboding. I suppose that is why I am so adamant and forthright in whatever I speak or write about. Father was very much into 'foreseeing' the future as well. Maybe he passed it on to one or two of his *mokopuna*.

Anyway, all of a sudden we'd see a mast and a launch would come into sight, then it would disappear, then rise up again out of the trough between the frothy cycle of waves breaking over the reef; the next launch appeared and then the next until they were all through that stretch of angry turmoil. They did have an alterative diversion; they could go right out beyond the reef where it wasn't breaking so bad, but that must have used more fuel perhaps. I don't really know why they didn't choose the cruisier passage.

When there was no wind, the reef was as calm and serene as a millpond.

The Whale

I have to tell you about this huge whale that washed up one day, way up on dry land above the sand-dunes, and up against the fence. There had been a 'monstrous' sea running which brought this gigantic whale in. As you can imagine, that must have been some storm!! I'm not sure now whether it was a sperm or a southern right whale. It was so big that we could see it from way back by the cutting onto the beach, about a mile away. It looked like a wrecked boat, and it was much bigger than any of the boats in the harbour. This was about 1946.

As soon as we heard about the stranding, our Teacher took us along to view this monster. On arrival at the scene we just stood in awe at the size of it. This whale was so big and high that none of us had a show of climbing onto it. Its skin was like leather. It must have been there for a day or two as it was dead as a door nail. Making matters more exciting, it died with its mouth open. Our Teacher took photos of us standing in its mouth, two of us at a time. Since then, when I've been in that area, I remember that event and feel sorry that I wasn't interested in keeping a photo. The Teacher showed them to us, but I can't remember wanting one. I'm sorry about that now.

On several trips back home, and knowing what I know now, I have gone to that exact spot and scratched around for bone or teeth, but to no avail; not a trace of any evidence. Somebody knew better than us at that time, and would have known the value of such a find. Nanny Ngaria had fireside stools which were the vertebrae from a whale's back-bone. They stood about 16-20 inches high, and the circumference was similar to the usual stool. That must have also been a massive whale.

Whales out in the bay were a common sight. We'd be sitting at our desks in the classroom watching them through the window, gliding across the bay squirting as if putting on a display for us kids. On other days the seals would perform, and the penguins had their turn as well. On arrival into our classrooms some mornings, we'd be entertained by a choir of penguins under our building. We didn't have frequent visits from them, but we always welcomed their presence. Then other times the seals on the rocks immediately below the school would render us their un-melodious barking. I think all this 'carry on' took place during their mating season.

Yes, we were so in tune with our *moana* and our *whenua*. The school and the school house were in a different place then [not very far from where they are today] and we had full view of the rocks and sea. A lovely ambience really. Sometimes I feel that our natural dispositions were controlled by the moods of the sea. When the sea was angry we were inclined to be a little unruly, and on calm days serenity would usually prevail. The sea has a strong pull. I found it quite strange when I went for a weekend with my friend who's Father managed Te Awatea Station. This place is inland, with no glimpse of the sea, and even though there are beautiful views of the lakes, without the sea I felt locked in and felt quite claustrophobic. I still long for the 'smell' of the sea; it's part of me. Luckily I'm not too far away from Mahia Beach.

This family [The Harringtons] as well as the Jacob family and a few others attended the little school at Te Awatea at the time. This school was probably one of the smallest ones in NZ. It was of course a 'sole charge' school which often looked so forlorn, yet making a strong statement as it sat defiantly on top of this little green nob on a hill in the bare paddock. The site is still visible from the main road, and from here one can soak up the most panoramic view of the lakes; Lake Huro, the mouth of the Lagoon at Te Awapatiki and all the *wahi-tapu* surrounding this beautiful vista.

David Holmes with mailbags outside the old post office when it was situated on beachfront, circa 1936.

Other Activities

How exciting it was to be in Waitangi on 'boat day'. I hadn't experienced this until my last two years before coming out to secondary school. I was then old enough to ride my horse to Waitangi by myself. Many people flocked to the wharf; the mail was usually the first item of freight to come off. These mailbags went directly to the Post Office, which was situated down along from where the Hotel Chathams Island is. This site was practically on the beach.

Mr. David Holmes was kept very busy as he operated the Mainfreight cartage around Waitangi – delivering to the shops, hotel, hospital, post office and goods of all descriptions to their destinations. He had a huge dray with about six draught horses pulling the load. Before my time, he used only two to pull the dray. It was actually an experience and entertaining listening to him commanding his team of horses. To make matters more exciting, he had names for each horse, and one could hear him conducting them from all over Waitangi. If only we had video cameras those days. Believe me, it was a grand sight and worth capturing. I'm sure the Holmes family must have photos of those wonderful moments. From 1930-1949 Constable Ryan Holmes (Dave's father) acted as the Registered Magistrate. That's history, isn't it?

I loved how whenever anyone had anything to celebrate, the whole island was expected to attend, and believe me, everyone who was able to go, went. We all enjoyed socializing, dancing, and music — in other words, having fun, whether it be a wedding or a picnic.

Another activity was playing euchre and housie on Friday nights at the school. We actually alternated the Friday nights with square dancing. This was wonderful entertainment. The dancing was superb. Uncle Charlie was the 'caller' for the square dancing, and the emcee as well. He was a champion at the job, a real Master of Ceremonies. All you older Islanders will remember how he and Aunty Cissie 'tripped the light fantastic'. They would have enjoyed the current TV programme "Dancing with the Stars". Eileen played the piano at times and an accordion player supplied the music for these evenings. The suppers at these 'dos' were something else. I don't think there was a woman on that Island who couldn't cook or bake. It was worth the while going just for the supper for some, the Oldies especially.

If we had an oversupply of food in our gardens we shared or swapped. No one went without, this was better than letting veggies go to seed. Down the road Mr. Donaldson (they also had a big family) had a real 'humdinger' of a garden, again everything flourished. One of the main advantages was his never-ending water supply. Yes, in the summer we often ran out of water if we relied on tank water only. We were always fascinated with his water pump sitting in the middle of his patch. You pumped the lever up and down to draw up the water which was artesian so pure and clear; the aqua-fir must have been so robust.

There would be very few people (if any) who could direct you to that water strata today. I still know the exact spot. What amazes me about this pure water is the fact that 90% of the creek water in Owenga is tinged with a brownish colour owing to the peat content in the ground. This bore must have gone down very deep, and then how did they bore or drill so deep in those days. Island ingenuity again.

Mr. Donaldson was also renowned for his homemade elderberry wine. He had hedges of the bushes. They say the wine had a kick like a draught horse. Those old 'diggers' certainly got their kicks out of that brew. Sometimes I wonder whether some of the wild berries, nectar, shoots and flowers of the *kawakawa* etc. had any 'happy side effects', because we were always a happy bunch of kids. Brings to mind the adage, "going on a trip without even leaving the farm." All jokes aside, a little further down the road was Uncle Charlie and Aunty Cissie's place. They had a top and bottom orchard with several bushes of red and black currants. These were ideal for jam-making, as well as the rest of the fruit in the orchards. There were glassy green gooseberries and red ones as well, and apples. All these fruits grew prolifically in this sheltered area. When I mention 'top' and 'bottom' orchard, it was because their house was sitting on top of a hill and directly below, almost on the beach, was the bottom orchard. This was truly another haven with thick vegetation of trees of all description, thus providing excellent shelter. As I have stressed, without shelter which is the most important factor, you're doomed. The prevailing winds have no mercy.

Because the twilights in the summer time were so long, there was always time in the evenings to play tennis as well as other sports. The young adults and older children played a lot of tennis on the school courts. These courts were situated below the school by the beach — a delightful place in the cool of a summers evening, with the beach and rocks just over the sand dunes, a hop step and jump away. Basketball (now called netball) was played on this court as well. The young kids preferred to play in the rock-pools, catching shrimps and cock-a-bullies. There were no transistor radios or games that they have today. That was probably why we played a lot. That must have been good for us, and it allowed us a lot of time for social interaction. We cared for one another. We knew where not to tread, as there are several *wahi tapu*. In fact, we often stumbled across exposed skulls and bones; we were taught to bury them again.

Our Culture

There was a kind of culture in Owenga. We were aware of stories handed down to us. Actually, I don't think "handed down" are the right words; we merely heard the adults talking. They never really sat us down and recited their stories, which I find a shame.

Our ethnicity or ancestry was never openly discussed; it was hardly a factor, although we (our family) knew we were Moriori. Our Elders spoke very quietly about our Moriori heritage. I guess they were still suffering the after-effects of the invasion like their parents before them. But despite not having enough vocal knowledge about our *whakapapa / hokopapa*, deep down inside of us we still felt and knew who we were, and we practised one of the most important customs of the Moriori, and that is *whakawhanaungatanga* — kindness and hospitality, and caring for our fellow men. Oppression is a hurtful thing that our fore-bearers suffered, and most found it hard to talk about. Only a Moriori "born and bred on Rekohu" would know.

And that is why I say, I grew up a Chatham Islander. I would have loved to have called this story "Growing up Moriori" but, as I have already said, this is a true rendition of *my* story and it would be rather remiss of me to do that. In fact, **no Moriori** was brought up as a Moriori, so to speak, in my time. Unlike other races, our generation was deprived of vocal local history.

My brothers and sisters (except Elaine) in the early 1980s.

Nevertheless, we did practise many daily customs; one that comes to mind is everyone sitting at the dinner table together. It was a great time for family togetherness. Before moving away from the table, we all asked, "May I leave the table?" I think that was pretty much the norm in every household. Father would always quote; "Manners maketh a man." Respecting your elders was strictly adhered to, as well as to be 'seen and not heard'. And the simple words; please, thank you, and excuse me were always part of our vocabulary.

New House

When Uncle Bunty returned from the War, and after marrying Myrtle, he dismantled our house, and that is when Father and I went to live with him and Aunty Myrtle. They married in St. Teresa's Catholic Church in Waitangi. Uncle Herbert and Aunty Nell [Gregory-Hunt] also married on the same day in the same place.

While the new house was being built, we lived up at Bob Jacob's place in Owenga. These are Aunty Dolly's parents and they were managing Manukau Station at the time. Aunty Nell and Uncle Herbert lived there with us for a time before going to Pitt Island. This was the cutest little cottage [previously owned by our Uncle Roger Riwai]. There were outer buildings consisting

Our brand new house, about 1947.

of bedrooms, a wash-house and wood-shed. It was well sheltered from the prevailing sou'westerly winds, even though it sits up on a hill. There were flax and other native shelter around it, and it is still standing there today.

We were only a stone's throw away from the beach and the rocks, probably a two minute walk. Those who know this place are aware of all the seafood that lies in abundance there. We fished for blue-cod off Louis Rock as well as over the other side off the flat rocks. The *kina* was plentiful there if you knew where to go, and the *paua* grazed in the shallow pools. Those days the deeper pools were simply littered with crayfish. When fishing for them we took our pick. We'd dangle a piece of rope or nylon stocking down into the pool and they all came out from under the ledge. When they grabbed the string, one only had to give a good quick pull and sometimes more than one would be clinging to the rope when we got them up onto the dry rocks!! You could go get those crays with your slippers on!! "That's fare dinkum." Sometimes they were so big, only one fitted into a kerosene tin, although we often preferred the smaller ones. There is also plenty of fish of all descriptions in the Bay between the Lois Rock and the flat rocks. I'd love to have that at my back door like we had then. Although as kids we'd rather have sausages. We'd almost cry when we had to have fish or *paua* for dinner 'again'.

When Peter Goomes was building the new house, Aunty Myrtle and I went to take his 'smoko' one Saturday morning. During the break he said, "By golly I wouldn't mind a crayfish for lunch." He knew the tide was just right, so off we went, grabbed a spear and a sugar bag and in no time we had pulled up this huge crayfish. We also got him some *paua* to take home that afternoon. By lunchtime the crayfish was on the table. I didn't like crayfish when I was young and Aunty didn't like it at the time either. He took it home. It was enough to feed a family.

It was an exciting time watching the new house being built. That wasn't a common scene in Owenga. It was the first house to go up over the last forty or fifty years, or maybe more. We were very happy living there. Uncle Bunty carted all his new furniture and household contents from the Waitangi wharf to Owenga on a large sledge pulled by a big team of bullocks. This was a massive task because the roads still weren't the best. I think it took him two to three days on the road. I do know that he stopped over at The Bar Twenty to feed and water the bullocks and of course as a comfort stop for him as well. He walked most of the time along side the sledge, so his weary legs would have needed a rest, and the load had to be checked and secured again. This is what life was like. He eventually arrived home with everything in tact. I marvel at what the men achieved in those rugged times, with 'roads' that were nothing more than tracks — deep ruts in the peaty soil.

We all had a new bedroom each and I often think of the pretty wallpaper that I had. We were only there for a matter of days and Father had his garden dug and ready to plant. He didn't put compost or anything of that sort in it first, as so many nutrients were in the soil. To keep or preserve his parsnips and carrots, he lept them in big boxes of sand. I've never since seen such big, sweet veggies. Next they made the smokehouse, then the chook-house and then the windmill stand and hey presto! We were in business again. The milking cow was already in the paddock with the horses. We were self-sufficient.

Aunty Eileen and cousin Reina Cotter picking paua.

Other Delicacies and Cooking Methods

*P*aua were also easy for us to cook because there were several ways of cooking them. I almost disliked *paua* as a kid because they were so often on the menu, especially when the men were fishing continuously during summer, and there'd be no one around to kill a mutton. *Paua* need very little cooking, they exude a lot of fluid during the cooking process, but more if they are left raw for a time. This is because they are haemophiliacs and they bleed profusely. If you were to leave a bowl of fresh shelled raw *paua* in a bigger container overnight, the next morning they'd be submerged in their own liquid known as 'blood.' A crayfish also has blood. It's the bluey-grey jelly like matter inside the raw crayfish, and when cooked it coagulates into spongy white pieces. I have enclosed recipes we used those days at the back of this book.

Aunty Myrtle's favourite way of having *paua* was sliced thinly then marinated in a brine of warm water, sugar and vinegar, with some thinly sliced spring onion. The accompaniment was basic buttered bread, pepper and salt. Now I fool around with them and make *paua* quiche and *paua* wontons ... something we had never heard of in our day.

When we had cod livers and roes, we rolled them in flour and fried them in very hot fat/oil. It was a matter of utilizing all our natural food resources. We learnt a little about cooking in oil when the Jurivich [Jury] family came to Owenga. They had big tins of the 'fair dinkum' olive oil. I still see their beautiful flawless skin, no doubt due to their diet. They cooked in oil most of the time.

When anyone in Owenga killed a cow or steer it was left to hang for a day or two, and then cut up and shared around the *whanau*. We pickled a lot of meat. Everyone owned a wooden barrel that was ideal for making the pickling brine in for curing the meat. That was what I call *real* corned beef. These barrels had many uses for making homebrew and water containers, etc.

During this era everyone in Owenga had chooks, so there were always roosters picking on one another and harassing the hens for the food. When they were big enough we culled them out. I now can't imagine myself chopping their heads off. Father held it on the chopping block and I chopped the head off – oh dear, how gruesome!! But that was life; some one had to do it. Uncle Bunty was away fishing and Aunty Myrtle was pregnant, and Father would not have involved her in anything quite so ghastly. At the time I thought nothing of it. We plucked them and stewed them using our own veggies, like carrots, onions, thyme and potatoes, and sometimes we made dumplings as well.

Tegal brand chickens weren't heard of then. The closest we ever got to a chicken was the old hens (the ones that had done their laying) and the feisty old roosters. After all that I must say, we did have a choice of other birds, and they were nothing but the best, but only the men-folk hunted those at the lakes. They were all there in abundance; the wild duck, swan, *weka*, *titi* and other birds.

Another delicacy for the Elders were the blind-eels. These were from the sea. I couldn't bare to look at the pinky slimy things, so I can't elaborate on them, although as I have already said, "The uglier the morsel from the *moana*, the sweeter the taste." I must say we did like the ordinary eels though. The

Mangahou creek was a good eeling place, as well as Hawaiki creek and of course the big lagoon up at Te Awapatiki.

Nanny Ngaria did a lot of her cooking in a camp oven on an outside fire, mainly when the fire had burnt down to embers. She baked the most beautiful madeira cakes and buns this way. She made hot cross buns one Easter in the same manner, by sitting the oven in a shallow hole with embers under and on top of it. Then she covered it with soil. Incidentally, that is how I learnt why the cross was on the bun. She told me briefly in her quiet manner the story about Easter. Needless to say, I had all the answers at the following Sunday school lesson, which we had every fortnight in our church, weather permitting, as the Minister had to come from Waitangi on horseback.

Nan cooked eels in the camp oven as well. First she placed clean pieces of sticks similar to kindling on the bottom of the oven in a criss-cross pattern to form a sort of rack. On this she placed the pieces of eel, salted them and added blobs of fat, put the lid on the oven then onto the embers until they cooked to a crispy texture. This was our favourite way of having them — *bon appétit*.

What I marvel at now is how our older people went about their chores without any fuss and bother. Time meant nothing and no one was in a hurry. I guess it is still a wee bit like that now. If they didn't have the goods to cook with, they improvised. Gosh I hate to admit it, but if I haven't got all the ingredients I just won't do it. I've grown out of that mode of making do of what you've got, probably because there's a shop down on the corner.

We did *Kanga pirau* — fermented corn, kanga pungarehu. This corn was boiled in water for hours with wood ashes. When the corn was cooked and soft to the pallet, you rubbed the husks off by shaking them vigorously in a colander. This is eaten the same way as the other corn — with cream and sugar, but this one doesn't have a smell about it. The oldies would say, "There's nothing wrong with the corn, it's the jockey on the top that's unhealthy and does the damage." Yes, the cream and sugar!

Nan could afford to do this with her corn because she grew it herself in her sheltered garden. They also put new potatoes in a bag [flour bag I think] and steeped them in a fast flowing creek like the corn. It didn't appeal to me, so I didn't see how they ate it – just like the corn I think – it was called *kotero*.

When I read about the annual Wild Food Fest they have on the Island today, I often wish I was there to present some of the food from *'mai ra ano'* – way back from when I was caring for our Nans. As I mentioned in my Preface, I originally wanted to convey to the Tamariki o te Kohanga Rea o Wharekauri nga kaimoana o matou kainga; the *kai* some may not know about or even eat these days. Some of what I mention here wasn't common practice. I was only lucky that I was Nanny Ngaria's caregiver, and that is how I learnt the old way. They were basic skills but these little 'gems' have taken me through life with ease, and above all – I appreciate what I've been taught and given as well as what life has dished out for me.

One of the oldtime morsels of the sea are the *kotoretore*, the common name being 'sunsets" to most of us, and in marine language the name is 'sea anemones'. They look like the flower of the same name when they are in full bloom in the pools. To me they are delicious, but one needs to know how to prepare and cook them, the method of cooking is simple. Please find more recipes at the back of this book. Then we also enjoyed the *ngakihi* limpid and the *taere* small mussel.

People like the late Bolan Goomes were great cooks. What I liked about those men and Bolan especially; they cooked with confidence and put feeling into their *mahi* (efforts). Some of the dishes he came-up with were 'one offs' to be sure. Bolan also had great food preservation skills. His kippered fish and eels that he bottled were 'to die for'. Yes, he certainly had a flare for cooking at picnics and other functions. His daughters are going to laugh when they read this because fond memories will come rushing back of his 'cordon bleu' cooking expertise.

I think back to when Grandma Hunt stayed with us on her way back to Pitt Island where she lived. She had been to New Zealand, and whist waiting for the seas to calm to cross the straights, she graced us with her presence. I must say, she certainly was a graceful lady. She taught us how to pick edible weeds to substitute, and as a change from the usual greens we cooked in our *kotutu*. I wondered why eat weeds when we have a garden full of veggies, but as usual we also had plenty of weeds. Some that come to mind are the stinging nettle, fat hen, *poroporo*, prince of whales feather, wild turnip and a bit of *puha*.

Her aim was to show us that these greens were as good as a dose of medicine, and how right she was. Sixty odd years later I'm perusing through the pages of a modern magazine and here it was — all the facts about the medicinal benefits of the common garden weeds. Now well-known companies are making huge profits in manufacturing these plants into medicines, in capsule and powder form, sold everywhere from supermarkets to health food shops. Our learned Elders knew it all. It must have been such an asset to have knowledge of these *rongoa* (medicines) when living in such isolation.

But that wasn't all, as she also brought some ready-to-eat cloves of garlic back from NZ. We had never heard of this pungent bulb before! She cut slits in a leg of mutton and slid cloves into it before roasting. It was foreign food to us, and I can't say I enjoyed it then. She also spoke of it being great for purifying the blood. How right she was! Interestingly, stinging nettle preparations are now renowned for ridding the body of toxins! When I now think back to that roast, it really must have been lovely. Today I would eat any meal flavoured with garlic. In later years I realised what a genius that lady was. On the Island and especially Pitt Island, it would have been so necessary for her to keep abreast with 'mother nature' — the *whenua* and the *moana*.

When I was about eleven years old I had a break-out of boils. They were horrid things. When they came to a head we had to persevere with having hot bread poultices put on them. This concoction helped to draw out the core — ouch! I was fortunate not to get them again. That was the only health issue I had as a child, and they can actually incapacitate you and confine you indoors. I bathed them in water in which gorse flowers had been boiled in, and after awhile there wasn't a sign of where they had been. Unfortunately, they can leave horrible scars — I was lucky. After that bout I continuously heard Fathers voice ringing in my ears, "That's what you get for not eating your veggies."

Father ate raw onions like eating apples — he swore by doing that it "frightened the flu away". I guess it wouldn't be any worse than going to bed with a clove of garlic in your sock! Mrs. Hill always had a peeled cut onion on her window sill above her sink bench; this was to ward off the flu, and it worked.

I'm sure we all have events and circumstances which occurred at some stage of our lives that have left indelible imprints on our minds. As I grow older and creakier these tales come flooding back, whereas years ago I couldn't have cared. But the people that populated my life have become very much alive in my memories.

Tree Carvings

In 1947-1948, an Anthropologist named Miss Jefferson came to explore the Moriori tree carvings known as the Dendroglyphs. We kids thought she was a bit "funny," however, out of respect for her I have since realized that the apt phrase for her was "a little eccentric." We seldom saw strangers, and were often suspicious of them. I guess isolation does that to a certain extent. Nevertheless, we grew to like her, and were always pleased when she came back to Owenga and called at the school to visit us. We always greeted her with a hearty "Good morning, Miss Jefferson." She was always in the same garb; an oil-skin coat, matching sou'wester and good ole gumboots ... appropriate attire for such arduous journeys around the Island, especially as it was winter. I don't know what possessed her to come during the winter months. I have no idea who it was that lent her the horse, her only mode of transport, but it was a fine looking black one and she really looked the part in the saddle. That bronco took her all around the Motu. It would have taken her months to ride around the places of interest to her. But, she has seen more of the Island than I have. When staying in remote parts of the Island, she pitched camp, but as soon as the inhabitants closest to where she was heard she was there, they would take her food and offer her lodgings.

She went back to the Island several times after her initial visit, and people were always pleased to see her. I think she went back 5 times between 1947 to 1954. She came back to Owenga several times to talk with Nanny Ngaria Martin [nee Riwai]. They became very good friends. I presume it was because Nan was ¾ cast Moriori and could still remember a lot of stories to tell her, some pertaining to the tree carvings as well. Nan was quietly spoken and I know Miss Jefferson would have found her to be honest and precise in every thing she told her. Nan was so humble and shy that it amazed us when she allowed her photo to be taken, and she features in the book Miss Jefferson published. In fact, that is the only photo in the book, the rest are Miss J's own drawings of the Dendroglyphs. The book she wrote is called *The Dendroglyphs of The Chatham Islands* and it is a very comprehensive account of the Moriori tree carvings.

More Memories

Around about this era we were all 'in the same boat' so to speak. Nobody was any better off than anyone else, and yet we never missed what we didn't have. Life carried on regardless. Because we didn't have electricity, the lucky ones had a generator that serviced the households. Most of us had lovely lamps that stood elegantly on the side boards, or some hung from the ceiling, or sitting on a table. They were treated with great care as they were exquisite really. We had to be ever so careful when refuelling them with kerosene in case we broke the delicate mantle. These were made of very fine mesh that fitted around the flame to enable incandescent lighting. As time moved on these lamps went out of production, and the Tilley lamp took over. These proved to be quite versatile because you could carry them around, even use them outside. Then along with these lamps came the introduction of the Tilley iron, for ironing clothes.

Talking about these kerosene lamps and irons, we received our kerosene in 24 gallon tins — two tins to a box. These boxes like most things had many uses. They were like a piece of furniture in a way. They were very solid and well made, like most things those days. These boxes were often used for seats. Upright they would serve as a chair, lying sideways they made good fireside seats. They were great for storage. I had one beside my bed with a pretty curtain hanging down the front. I sat my candlestick on it, much better than having the candle on the drawer when one had to reach out to put it out. As I mention these boxes, I marvel at what we utilized those days. For instance, there were no public rubbish dumps in those days, yet I don't think we had much to dump. Most of us had our own rubbish holes, and the only things we discarded were unusable tins and bottles.

We had wax matches then, and they were about one inch long and stayed alight for much longer than these wooden ones today. Dripping wax on things was a nuisance. We were always careful not to drip wax on our records, the ones we played on a gramophone. We had a wind-up gramophone and thrashed the same records over and over. We had fun trying to imitate the songsters of the day. Some songs at the time were sung by Gene Autrey, Tex Morton, Patty Paige, and Doris Day. We had our favourites. The boys sort of favoured the cowboy songs, today known as Country Music. There was quite a bit of amateur yodelling happening as well. We tried to copy the music recorded on the radio programme called the Hit Parade and all the latest hits. My sisters and I made quite a good job of the song "Down in the Valley".

We found a few good blackberry bushes in a nearby paddock. In season, we'd go with 'billies' made from 7lb. golden syrup tins. We started off with our billies full and by the time we got home we'd eaten half of them. We were lucky to get four bottles of jam. Sometimes when we ran out of preserving jars, the men folk would cut the tops off the beer bottles. I think they did it by heating a round piece of wire in the fire and then putting it around the neck of the bottle. We sealed our jams and other preserves with melted wax (the proper wax for this purpose).

Mushrooms in season grew literally everywhere in this paddock as well. We had fun picking them and then kicking the big 'puffballs' around the paddock. As I said earlier, our stoves were burning all day, so we would just throw them on the top of the stove like cooking on a hot plate today, sprinkle a bit of salt on them and yum – Jamie Oliver, eat your heart out. The kettle was continuously on the boil too, and a pot of tea brewed with this water was so satisfying and quenching. Mind you, we used tea leaves then, as teabags weren't invented. No one stopped to talk without going inside for a 'cuppa'. This was a ritual. Hospitality was a natural practice everywhere, perhaps because we didn't really go too far away from our comfort zones, and we always kept in close contact.

As I mentioned, social gatherings were common, and this was so good for the children. Whenever there was something happening it more than often took place at the school. This was the true epitome of *whakawhanaungatanga* and *manaakitanga* (togetherness and caring), which is a very important tenet of Maori/Moriori *tikanga*. I've often thought that going away to school and away from this close knit environment was another reason why I suffered so much with homesickness. I suppose it would be fair to say that we knew every one and everyone elses business.

Those of us who were Moriori knew who we were, and the white people also knew their lineage. Our Grannies were friends with everyone. Ethnicity wasn't mentioned. We were simply Chatham Islanders, at the same time bearing in mind who we really were.

Grandma and Grand-Dad

I'm thinking of Grandma Hough again – she had a lovely garden. There was a cute little box hedge running up both sides of the front path. She had fruit trees galore all growing in sheltered areas, and in this same place she grew a mass of gladioli of many different colours. What a pretty show they made through the kitchen window. This was the cutest two-storied house. This lovely cottage is one of the oldest houses in Waitangi that is still inhabited by new owners. It is gratifying to know that it is still loved. I am so pleased to know that it is still lived in and cared for.

The other charming old homestead is also situated in Waitangi; a large two-storied house build of kauri wood in 1882. It is the biggest house on the island. The Holmes family owned this place from 1926 to sometime in the early 1990s. From 1930-1949, Constable Ryan Holmes (David's father) was our Resident Magistrate.

Grandma also looked after the Catholic Priest. His little cottage and the church [St. Teresa's] was only a stones throw from her house. I was always scared of the 'perpetual light' that glowed in the church at night. On the way home from the pictures on a Saturday night we'd put on a bit of a spurt when passing.

Grand-dad spent many a day up at the farm called Big Bush up past Te One. He would ride there and back in a day. He often killed and dressed a mutton up there and rode back the next day to cut it down and bring it home in his *pikau* bag. I have never known such a 'laid back' gentle man.

Grandma always had a joint of cold meat in the meat safe. Every home had a meat safe; they were as important as the house itself. They were always hung in the coolest part where the air could flow cross-currently through it. If you had the exact spot it was nearly as good as a fridge. Cold meat from the meat safe tasted delicious. In fact, every time when I went back to Uncle Bunty's the first place I made for was the safe, and sure enough they'd have some cold meat and other succulent morsels in their typical Chatham larder/pantry.

The food on the Island seemed to taste so much nicer. I dug out some carrots from Charlie's garden last time I was home — they were so sweet and I truly do think it's the soil and probably the climate. As I keep on saying, the Island has great potential for vegetable growing, and I still think that berries would grow great there as well. Okay, I am aware of getting produce to the markets in excellent condition, but imagine a sign reading "Fresh organic vegetables and berries from the Chatham Islands." Wouldn't that create a stampede!! Again, the crippling problem would be the freight.

Talking about meat safes, there were also the big ones that stood a few feet away from the houses. They could accommodate a whole beast. This little out-building had all the hooks and gambles, chopping block and other necessary tools such as saws and knives. Some even had water laid on or a water tap close by.

This brings back to mind another horrific scare I had as a child. This experience took place at Manukau Station when I was about nine years old. I was having a peep at the beast hanging in this big safe and feeling it to see if it was still warm when the door slammed shut. I was rather apprehensive about touching this huge beast that hung from the rails to the floor, but inquisitiveness took over. I must have screamed till I was 'blue in the face'. After what seemed like a life-time the door opened. One of the Station-hands went past previously and shut/locked the door. To this day I really never bothered to find out whether it was done purposely or innocently. However, that fiasco has left me with a life-long fear called claustrophobia. I cannot sit in a small room with the door shut. I suffered terribly when flying back to the Chathams on a Metro plane, one of those small pencil-liners. I was on the verge of collapsing with anxiety attacks; it wasn't until we were half way across that I ceased perspiring. The same trauma happened when I went to Wellington for an MRI scan. I just went into 'collapse mode.' The intense closeness inside that capsule was far too overwhelming for me. Needless to say, the magnetic resonating imaging was not fully satisfactory. What a waste of a one day trip to Wellington. Believe me, it's a dreadful phobia to have, as bad as spider phobia.

I always marvelled at the pace these old people went about doing things, nothing was a bother yet they never had the modern conveniences that we have today. I have recently realized why, all through my life I have gravitated towards the Elders, this is probably because I had spent my young life around them constantly.

Inlet on the way to Port Hutt, with the Clears in foreground and background.

Race Day on Chatham Island, circa early 1930s.

The Races

The annual two-day race meetings were the most important events of the year. I'm sure all those who were able to be there attended. Most of us kids didn't start going until the roads were formed. Father always went because he trained horses. He also trained horses for people from other parts of the Island. He ran his horses on Clough's beach and the long beach that sweeps around Hanson Bay. I remember a horse called "Naumai" belonging to the Tuuta family from Te Marama up past Te One. Young Charlie always went to the races in later years when I was at boarding school. He was a top jockey – one of the best jockeys the Island produced. I always received letters from home telling me of his successes. They had a race horse called "Lucky Star" in those days. Charlie rode three winners in one day at one meeting. These meetings were held between Christmas and New Year, so all the high school students were home for their holidays.

Race day was an opportunity for the women to adorn their finery, enhanced with hats and matching gloves and shoes, and of course the appropriate hosiery. Those days the nylon stockings had a seam running straight up the middle back of the leg. Oo-la-la! The majority of the men wore their best attire too; some wore ties and polished shoes and looked very dapper.

Race Day riders, late 1950s.

The grandstand wasn't big enough to accommodate everyone, so the centre inside the course became a huge gathering venue, like a picnic area. People made a semi circle by parking their vehicles close and tidy beside each other. This created a close-knit togetherness. Marquees were erected, ground covers laid out, and some even had picnic tables and chairs. Several race-goers stayed on and partied into the night.

The second day was a bit different. There wasn't as much on-course activity or festivities like the previous day, mainly because this night was 'the night' for socializing, dancing and of course, the presentation of some of the trophies. This was a special night for Owners and Trainers. I don't think I'd be wrong in saying that this was the biggest night of the year that everyone looked forward to, a night of 'razza-matazz'. Again, everyone turned out dressed to kill. The Waitangi Hall was bursting at the seams. The womenfolk had the opportunity again to wear their beautiful dresses and accessories, and let me add, there were many very good-looking and well-dressed people on the Islands. Dancing was very popular all over the Islands, as well as music and singing. At the first race meeting I attended I couldn't stop gazing at some of the hats the women were wearing. One particular hat still stands out in my minds eye. It was a fawnish colour with a small bunch of imitation berries and fruit pinned elegantly on the side of it. A touch of class, and it suited the 'classy lady' who wore it. Whenever something like that caught my eye I would always think, "When I grow-up I'm going to get me one of those." Anyone can dream!

I must speak of the food and refreshments on the first day. The food was laid out like a huge smorgasbord, and people simply moved from car to car socializing, nibbling from here and there in between a 'nip' of this and a 'swig' of that. Happy punters everywhere.

Sadly, those days have long gone. Anyone my age or older must surely miss those times. Those lovely moments must have left a void for some of our older Islanders.

Yes I speak of all this cuisine, but I seldom ate any of what I'm writing about. Just like kids of today, we rather preferred

Another Race Day scene, early 1950s.

'rubbish' and why not ... while we were in town we tried to make the best of it. Now the tables have turned and I hunger for the foods of our Island, hence the reason why I can't stop raving on about it. Maybe it's a phase in ones old age. I have a funny feeling that only a Chatham Islander could perhaps enjoy the details in this book, but by the same token, I do wish it will interest others. There is such a vast difference between those days and now, which I find interesting. Life's a whole new ball game today, and that applies to most places.

I have mentioned before how I tire of opening up a book about the Chathams and it's all about the Moriori Tree Carvings, the Invasion, the Maori and the gruesome consequences. Even though I am *tuturu* (a real) Moriori and well aware of the history and the *whakapapa* of the Islanders, I am steering clear of that because there are too many questions that *need* to be answered yet, before things get better. You can't play with fire and walk away without getting burnt. And you can rest assured that this is a *true* rendition of my childhood life growing up a Chatham Islander. I have yet to find out who as a Moriori actually grew-up as one. By this I mean practising the *true kawa and tikanga* and the Moriori language, and *living it*. Nobody that I know of, except our Nans, and I am not about to talk a lot of rubbish just to try and authenticate a Moriori upbringing. I am not a professional writer, nor am I a 'bull-dust' storyteller. Anyone my age and older, who grew up on the Chatham Islands will agree, 'we were all one' for in spite of all of us knowing our ethnicity, we lived together beautifully.

Other Delicacies and Cooking Methods 137

White-baiting in Te Whanga Lagoon. Sometimes one scoop measured half a bucket!

Aunties Cissie, Gladys, and Eileen with teachers' girls and Roger Prece on rocks in Owenga, circa 1949.

School Days

At school the boys had woodwork and the girls did a variety of handcrafts. We had a machine that drilled holes in *paua* shells. For awhile we had a fad for making *paua* shell buttons and brooches. Eventually I couldn't stand even looking at another button. Years after I wished I had kept some, especially when *paua* shell became the 'in thing' again. We had a lot of shells to work with. We picked shells from our special places; they were pieces that had been washed over and over by the tide so they looked as if they had been 'tumbled' like they do at the factories. It amazes me to see the price they put on *paua* shell jewellery today.

During my primary school days, I think we had three Principals: Mr. Wotherspoon, Mr. Bowkett and Mr. Amundsden. Mr. Wotherspoon married an Owenga woman — she was Annie Nielson. He taught in Kaingaroa before coming to Owenga. The school was sole-charge, meaning it warranted only one teacher, this being determined by the roll. All the schools on the Island adhered to the National Education Curriculum. At that time, there were five schools on the Chathams; Te One, Kaingaroa, Te Kai Rakau, Te Awatea and Owenga. Te Awatea functioned now and then, depending on pupil availability. In earlier times, I believe Matarakau had a school as well. There was also a school on Pitt Island, and they still have a school there today.

Mr. Bowkett was a very nice man and teacher, and was well-liked in the community. His wife was also lovely; she taught us sewing and arts and crafts. They had two school-aged girls, Judith and Roslyn. I have in the past seen the name Bowkett appear on TV credits and in other media, and wondered if there could be a connection.

By the time I was a pre-teen in Standard 5 and 6 (now referred to as year 7 and 8), our teacher was Mr. Amundsden. I am convinced that Mr. Amunsden didn't care whether we sank or swam. He was more interested in archaeology than our education. He was in this environmental sphere (in his element) because he had no one keeping tabs on him, and no Inspector about to appear. When the school Inspectors were about to visit, there was always plenty of time to prepare.

When the tides were low, the class walked from below our school way along to Clough's creek hunting for Moriori curios and artefacts. Most of us objected to scratching around for anything suspicious-looking, but we were ignored by him. We had been taught from an early age that to dig around the sand hills was not acceptable. We knew that if we came across bones or sculls, we were to bury them again after all, they were our ancestors.

However, after a lot of non-cooperation, he changed tactics. We then ventured onto rock-pooling, but if the tide was high he would send us out to play 'rounders' (similar to soft-ball). While we played in the field, he was in his hut bagging up his curios and things. I think he may have also been a 'ham radio' operator. If the weather was inclement we did artwork. All these activities were fun to us, and much better than school work. Little did we realize it was doing us an injustice and there was no formal education going on. In later years, I understood that I certainly was a victim of a negligent teacher.

One day after one of our escapades along the beach, Father asked, "What did you do at school today?" It was quite uncanny; he hadn't left our house but he knew we had been fossicking in the sand hills. He said he could 'see' something on me. I had no idea what he meant. He wouldn't let me have anything to eat until I washed up. Then the inevitable happened ... the lecture was all on, as he felt it was best for me to be told (again) about these things: *nga tikanga o matou kainga*, the customs of our place. Father was so spooky at times. He was like a mind-reader. He certainly had accurate premonitions.

Unfortunately for me, I never learnt much in those last two years with Mr. Amundsden. He certainly didn't prepare me for what was to come — secondary school. It was 1952 when I went away to school in Napier, and I was just a young teenager. I am not writing about anyone else, this story is about what life was like for *me*. I definitely was not up to 'standard' on arrival at school. I had an extremely hard row to hoe to catch up to the others. I was bereft of hope and feeling unhappy for not being able to conform. He even had the audacity to recommend I sit for the prestigious Ngarimu scholarship. Of course I failed miserably. He never gave me any 'prepping' or previous assistance. On reading the exam paper, it was like a foreign language. I felt like I had been pushed out to sea in a dinghy with no oars. Luckily the Nuns in Napier nurtured me later and gave me one-on-one instruction until I caught up.

The Author in 1971.

Attending School In Napier

My childhood eventually came to a close, and it was on the north island of New Zealand where I eventually met my husband Paul Mete in 1956 and had a family, and still live today. I left Chatham Island and moved to Napier in Hawkes Bay to attend school when I was only 13-14 years old. It was my very first time away from home. I flew out on a TEAL Flying Boat; Tasman Empire Airways Limited. We landed in Evans Bay in Wellington. Well!! The sight of this massive city was almost too much for me to absorb; everything was so overwhelming. I really did feel like a fish out of water. Aunty Stella was there to meet me and whisked me off to our lodgings, the People's Palace in the city. I couldn't sleep properly that night; I kept looking out the window down onto the traffic and the people with awe, all going to and fro. I was going dizzy. Now that's what I would call a "muri-back native"!!

I remember the next day we went on the railcar north to Wairoa, and that was another experience. We travelled all the way back to Rangiahua. When school started, I travelled from Wairoa back down to Napier on a bus called the "Service Car". I have no idea how many times I made use of the bags from behind the seats along that windy road! Oh dear, I was sure out of my realm and alone on this trip. The Head Prefect was at the Napier bus depot to meet me, and we taxied back out to school. I arrived at school a few days late.

I knew in advance that St. Joseph's Maori Girls College was staffed by Nuns. I had seen a Nun in a white habit, as they staffed our Island Hospital back home, but nobody had warned me that these ones were in "black habits" from head to toe ... another culture shock. They reminded me of the big penguins I had just left behind.

Being in this big 3rd Form Dormitory with 30 other homesick girls also away from their homes and comfort zones was so daunting – Aue! *Ka pamai te aroha me te pouri o taku ngakau mo taku Papa me taku kainga ka maringi noa nga roimata.* Oh dear, the pain of homesickness was so intense, and missing Father and my Island home was almost unbearable that I cried every night for the first month. I missed Father so much that I found it hard to concentrate. But I did survive, and I am lucky that my grandparents were always an omnipresent force in my life no matter where the years took me. The feelings are still the same today. One of my best friends was Minna Clair (nee Puanaki), and we still see each other in town occasionally.

The nuns were specialists in their fields and all had teaching degrees, some having been awarded with MBE, OBE, and QSO. They were very devoted to their teaching subjects. We did have one lay teacher – she was our Maori language and cultural tutor. Our physical education teacher was also a local Napier man. Then we had this lovely man who was our marching instructor who had recently retired from the Army at the time. We had three marching squads and our own drum corps. Our drummers were 'the talk of the town'. No one could equal the Maori girls from SJC with their built-in rhythm – "Sussex by the Sea" rings in my ears at the thought of them. We were highly commended wherever we marched. There was always a scramble for the daily paper the day after an event, just to read the accolades. Our biggest highlight was the Hastings Blossom Festival in September. We really enjoyed putting on a marching display here, and we always received lots of prizes. Free hot dogs and things were so appreciated. During my last year there, we 'Trooped The Colour in Wairoa' as part of the entertainment for some important event they had at that time.

Always we were treated to an array of 'eats'. We hadn't heard of the word 'smorgasbord' in those days — but that is what it was, and of course, we Maori girls were always hungry. Believe me, we weren't fed like how they are today at boarding schools, and we never were allowed to eat on the buses, but we had nothing to eat while travelling anyway. We only had one shilling whenever we went anywhere. However, they were great learning times, and eating far less than what we were used to didn't do us any harm. We were so used to eating what we wanted to at home that part of our homesickness was caused by feeling hungry most of the time. I'm sure my stomach thought my throat was cut for the first term. We did have a food cupboard in the refectory, where anything sent from home was kept until such time that the Nun on duty would oblige. Sometimes Maori bread would be in that cupboard for over a week. By the time the girl(s) concerned were allowed to have it, it was quite stale — but it was still 'choice' to us.

We were often asked to sing at certain events in Napier at the request of the Napier City Council. Sometimes it may have been only the Kapa Haka group required, and they also excelled. The other big annual event was the broadcast over the National Radio 2YA which was recorded in the Napier Studio. St. Joseph's was renowned (and still is) for their singing and music. Those days we had a music teaching Nun who devoted every day, except the weekends, to this subject. She taught the piano, violin, singing and voice training to all the girls who were interested, plus some outside pupils from around Green Meadows and Taradale. She was a real taskmaster and stood for no 'humbug'. Only those who qualified were in the College Choir.

My music fees were paid for, but I just wasn't interested. In spite of having a piano at home which Aunty Myrtle and Aunty Eileen played often, and I also liked fooling around on it, I still didn't grab the opportunity when I had it in my lap. I am so sorry now. I vividly remember one sister scolding me, "You bold, brazen hussy — how dare you let your parents down like this!" Her name was Sister Mary Channel, a forerunner to the famous Sister Mary Leo. Because of her devotion to this school, eventually it went onto making 'records', then onto tapes and CDs.

I was fortunate to have them realize my plight. Since everything was like a foreign language to me once arriving in Mainland New Zealand, it took such a long time of concentration to catch up, and I had so many other issues to deal with like homesickness and cultural differences. Being the learned person that she was, my Tutoring Nun was caring and thoughtful. After a short time I felt less belittled or ashamed. She would say to the rest of the class, "Valerie comes from a small isolated Island where they didn't always have a teacher, so this is why I spend time with her." We did have a teacher, but she was too polite to say he was the cause of my failure. She made me feel good instead of feeling dumb, and I soon made lifelong friends, and eventually enjoyed my years there.

Throughout my life, I often think of what the Nuns taught us, and I am eternally thankful for having been sent to St. Joseph's Maori Girls College in Napier, under the tutelage of those wonderful Nuns. Some were stricter than others, and some were a bit staid and old fashioned. I remember when I was about 16 years old, in 'Form 5', some of us girls plucked our eyebrows. Well, we were almost expelled. I really don't know how they noticed our eyebrows because we only shaped them. The Reverend Mother called us "hussies" and "did we realize we looked like street girls?" Aue!! It's a good thing she's not here today to see the current trends.

We were often accused of being 'boy-crazy'. We weren't even allowed to look out the window when the gardener walked past! And he was about 60!! Whistling or crossing our legs over our knees wasn't lady-like. If we were out on the lawn on a Sunday reading, we had to face towards the school just in case some boys went past and distracted us!

What we did enjoy was going up to the Seminary in Greenmeadows where these young men trained to become Priests. On the odd occasion, we went there and celebrated a Saint's Feast Day with the Brothers. Luckily for us, we didn't have to write essays about our visit and the service. I would not have been able to do so, as most of us girls were busy ogling our eyes at the young men. This sort of behaviour was forbidden, but we couldn't help it. I remember looking at this handsome Brother, he lifted his head up and looked me straight in the eyes as if he could read my mind. I have never seen a bloke blush like that since. Every time I saw him after that we just stared at each other. Wasn't that naughty? I thought about being a Nun after that!! – No, only joking. At the end of the day, the Nuns looked upon us as their *whanau*. Our old Rev. Mother who was at the Reunion I attended a few years later referred to us 'old girls' as her *mokopuna*. She went around speaking to us individually, asking what career did we pursue ... were we teaching, nursing or doing secretarial work for the Government like what they had drummed into us. Surprisingly, she was happy enough to learn that we were great mothers and good wives.

Although I attended that school as a non-Catholic, I will always respect their Mass, Benediction, Rosary and everything else pertaining to their way of worship. I'd go to Sunday Mass sometimes when I went to Napier to visit my *mokopuna* while she was a pupil there. When the girls sing those hymns, it's awesome. During my time, we recited the Mass in Latin in my first year: *Dominus vobiscum- Deo Gratias*. After the Chathams, this is one of the most important periods in my life, because I am thankful for how the Nuns moulded me, this Chatham Island girl, into a young woman — quite a transformation from chopping heads off fish and roosters!!

I vowed I'd never go back to the Island until I was well and truly an adult, and guess what? I adhered to my word. After school in Napier, I got a job as a J.R. (Junior Assistant) at a primary school in Whakaki in northern Hawkes Bay. I was 'on my way' to Teaching College. One day my friend invited me to the theatre in Nuhaka, which was a very busy little town back then. It was a set up, because her boyfriend's cousin came too, and we became a foursome. This cousin, Paul, later became my husband. In 1960, we took a holiday back to Chatham with our first two children, Paul and Jan. Years later, after Donna was born, we all moved back to the Chatham Islands in 1968.

Our Last Trip Home

It was 1968 when my late husband Paul and I took our three children back to the Island to stay awhile. This was about the middle of the crayfish boom. Paul left from Gisborne with my stepfather John Harvey (the Skipper), Graham and Allan (two of my brothers), and the engineer George Jolly on the fishing boat "Silver Dawn" that had been on the slip. The kids and I flew over from Wellington on a Bristol Freighter. This big plane transported everything and anything from a needle to a cow. It carried 20 passengers and about ½ ton of freight on each trip.

Val and Paul with their three children, 1967.

The landing strip was at Hapupu, an out-of-the-way place, but I believe it provided the most suitable strip of land for a runway. It was quite away out in the sticks. It must have created havoc for the ground staff and flight personnel at the best of times. Because there was no road or vehicle access to and from the main road to this airstrip, passengers and freight were ferried across the Lagoon to the main road. The length of that crossing was about four miles. We were then driven onto Waitangi (the main township) in the same vehicle. This Moggy was a big GMC truck which was fitted with a passenger capsule, as well as a suitable area for the mail freight and luggage.

The depth of the Lagoon crossing generally varied according to the tide patterns, certain winds and changeable weather. What a great experience it was for our children. They loved crossing the lake in the GMC. It was quite different to the first time we took them over. That time we flew on a Flying Boat, a Sunderland. They thought we were drowning when we hit the Lagoon with a loud splash [a much different part of the Lagoon where the water is much deeper] and while the plane taxied across the water, all one could see were bubbles and water through the port holes. I must say, that can be quite frightening for the uninitiated.

However getting back to the Moggy, on a calm day like it was when we arrived there, you could see the flounders flapping and scuttling on the sandy lake bed. The kids were bewildered. The driver took everything in his stride; nothing bothered him. He was an Islander who grew up on the lakes of Rekohu, and was very capable of navigating or fording the Lagoon.

The depot for unloading passengers and luggage, mail and freight was outside the Post office. From that point passengers were met and collected by family and friends. The sojourn may not have been too comfortable for the faint-hearted, or ladies in nice skirts and swanky footwear. Nevertheless, one needed to prepare when flying to the Island in those days, because you never knew what weather conditions you were flying into. Mind

Our Last Trip Home   151

Uncle "Ath" in younger years with two sons Gary and Wayne while docking at the Brook.

you, some of the Island women travelled in jazzy gear. They keep up with fashion over there.

We settled in Owenga, staying with Aunty Eileen and Uncle Athol, and their sons Gary and Wayne until such time that we had a place of our own. We enjoyed being there and the kids only had to go through the fence to school. They were great times ... the days our kids will never forget. We were in the bosom of my *whanau*.

Uncle Bunty had a wee batch built for us that was immediately across from Ferons Fish Factory. The builders who built the Factory were still in Owenga being inundated with building jobs for several people. I think they had other carpentering work that kept them there for more than two or three years after building the factory. We were lucky that Uncle Bunty was able to pull strings, and our batch was done in record time.

Paul secured a job at Ferons the day after we arrived — that was a bonus. After a while he graduated to managing the Factory, and our last year on the Island he went cray-fishing with

Our batch in Owenga in 1968, which has had an extension built on since.

Uncle Charlie on the boat called the "Owenga 8". Yovich & Hopkins had eight fishing boats there, they were all identical, and they were all called the Owengas – numbering from 1 to 8. Some afternoons after school our son and his friend would grab the dinghy and row their hearts out. I thought 'one day he's going to be a fisherman' but, no such luck – he qualified as a panel-beater instead.

In a short space of time, several crayfish Factories sprung into production. There were four in Owenga namely; Ferons, Ascots, Skeggs and Yovich & Hopkins. There was also one in Kaingaroa, Port Hutt, Waitangi and Pitt Island. The population of Owenga soared to capacity with fishermen and their families arriving, some with caravans as well. Most stayed in the accommodations. Yovich & Hopkins had workers' huts down where The Roaring Forty's is today, and they ate in the Factory dining room which was the top story of the fish shed. The other factories had their own accommodations.

Consequently the school roll doubled during this time. This being a sole charge school meant the Teacher needed help. After settling into our little place, I assisted at the school for a while. Those were great days, and I did enjoy being back in my old classroom in a totally different capacity, and mixing with the children of that generation. Those were the days. Everyone was so busy you hardly had time to 'swing around' as we were all working.

Unfortunately, I became ill and had to be flown out to Christchurch Hospital on a mercy flight. I had developed minor heart problems way back then in 1971. I was advised to return to Hawkes Bay as it was well known amongst the medical fraternity that we had one of the best Heart Specialists in NZ to perhaps take care of me. Luckily, we never sold our house on the Mainland, so with great reluctance and sadness we wended our way back to Nuhaka. My husband liked being on the Island so much that he could have spent the rest of his days there, and the kids were the same. Our son would have been ready for High School a short time after anyway. There would be no more rowing way out in the Owenga Bay in a dinghy with his mate [until they were out of sight] and scaring the daylights out of me. We slowly eased our way back into the more organized lifestyle.

I would really like to 'go on' about those happy times we all had back there in Owenga, but this story is *about me* while "*Growing up a Chatham Islander.*" I'd like to write about the social functions we had in the factory recreation room and in the summer months — down in our "Corral", a clearing in a plantation where we had haangis and barbeques. The fishermen built a floor in there so the people could dance.

Down in our 'Corral'. Paul is on guitar and Doug Kedgley on accordion.

They also built circular seating. But, that's another story and I hope that one day one of my children will pick up where I leave off and write their impressions of living and roaming around Owenga like the wild flowers of Rekohu.

The Airport today is a far cry from the Bristol Freighter era. It is situated in a totally different area, and is now a very bustling place for such a small population, with flights in and out almost on a daily basis, plus a small plane that services Pitt Island regularly.

It brings back memories of when we were kids and heard an airoplane flying around. Even though we couldn't see it through the clouds, we got a thrill. We'd all jump up out of our desks and run outside, hoping for a climpse. They were probably Air Force planes on air exercises. This is what that chapter of life on the Chathams was about. That was then – this is now.

Aunty Stella on way back to New Zealand on a Bristol Freighter, circa 1984.

Yes, I'm pleased our family had that opportunity to experience that trip of a lifetime. There certainly are vast differences from then to now on the Island. Today with regular flights and shipping to and from the Chathams the school children and parents come out to mainland NZ during their holidays — some flying further afield to places out of the country. Their options are now unlimited. They are not really disadvantaged living there, other than the cost of travel. However, that is the price one pays for living on such a beautiful island. Many dignatories, members of Parliament, botanists, scientists, Dept of Conservation personnel visit regularly. When I was in Wellington Hospital in February 2011, my heart specialist had recently returned from ten days on the Island with his family. They loved it. He had nothing but praise for the hospitality and food whilst staying at the Hotel Chathams.

When flying into the Island now, and looking down onto the shape of it, the lagoon and the necklace of lakes surrounding the lagoon, and the sea that surrounds it like a guardian — it is to me "the most beautiful sight to behold". I have recently heard that Owenga is coming alive again. That was like music to my ears. We had the most vibrant village and it could happen again especially if the young people return. I feel sure the older folk will join in and support.

Cropping The Islands

About six or seven years ago, I attended a meeting of the Moriori Trust Board on the Chatham Islands where I mentioned how well many crop plants flourished in the Island environment, especially in Kaingaroa where we own the Kaingaroa Station, with the hope that they may at least consider diversifying from sheep and cattle farming to perhaps a bit of cropping. I knew it would be a labour intensive task, but nothing happens without hard work – 'no pain no gain'. I thought of freight costs as well as fluctuating prices of the product, and how it would be better to have 'two irons in the fire' than none at all. However, I may as well have been talking to myself. My suggestion to the Iwi fell on deaf ears, and I was completely ignored. My proposal wasn't even minuted.

I can't help but think about the world today, and survival ideas for the Chathams. The fruits that the Weizner Brothers grew there are now known as 'exotic' fruits, and I thought they may have given it some thought. The last time I spotted gooseberries in the super-market they were $7.00 per punnet, not even enough for a pie for one person, and the punnet was smaller than a strawberry one. I am also aware that red and black currants are valuable for ridding the body of toxins, and they also cost a leg and an arm, if one is lucky enough to find them in the shops. They actually flourish on the Chathams.

It is inevitable that the world is consuming less meat products. I wonder why more Nuhaka farmers here where I now live aren't diversifying from beef and lamb to cropping. Mind you only a small percentage of the land is cropped, but it has proven to be profitable. I live in a rural area and all around me are sweetcorn, maize and squash pumpkins in season. Fifty years ago, one wouldn't dare to imagine this happening.

Today the way of the world is modification, so wouldn't it make sense to grow what is suitable for the Island conditions? But when thinking of the Moriori Iwi, you need manpower as nothing happens by just talking — 'procrastination is the thief of time.'

I must say the meat on the Island is something else. I'm not being bias, but it is simply the best, and again organic. By the same token I am not saying sheep and cattle farming are uneconomical, and I am aware of price fluctuations, so go for it if it's viable.

These days it would be a risky venture to purchase a farm on the Chatham Islands unless you really know what you're doing. It is all about feasibility, governance and management. One would need to look at the advantages and disadvantages, and the pros and cons — and there are many. To run a profitable farm today, it has to be run like any other business. The bookwork is as essential as the manual work, especially if you are accountable to an Iwi or any other group of owners. Another disadvantage on the Island is the rampant growth of gorse. Unless this is kept under control, you'll loose the plot. Then there's animal husbandry soil and pasture experience one needs to be au fait with. On the Chatham Islands the manual efforts are thrice as hard to contend with, as well as the diligence to keep going. And then there is the cost of freight, which is actually a logistical nightmare at times.

I admire and congratulate those farmers who run a good farm property on the Island. On my last visit home, I went to the South Coast to the 'Release of the Tui'. What a beautiful place. So much breaking-in and clearing of the land has been done there and it's a credit to the hard work of the Tuanui and Horler families. You deserve the lovely picturesque landscape. The lovely green tracts of land that reach out to the rocks and the sea is picture book stuff indeed. *Kia Kaha Koutou* (carry on with the great work).

Recently several people told me that the "Country Calendar" programme that aired on a Saturday evening was about farming on the Chathams, and that it was "the best programme they've seen about the Chatham Islands." It was about the Tuanui and Horler families. Isn't that great! I am also aware of other lovely properties on the Island like Owenga Station, Waitangi West and Wharekauri.

I'm still on about gardens — I suppose it's because every time I think of my childhood I remember these lovely gardens. I can't imagine us having survived without them; they were the essential and primary basis of our lives. Aunty Cissies flower garden was botanical. The majestic hollyhocks, delphiniums and the aquilegia (Grannies bonnets) growing along the pathway were a welcoming sight. I saw the Tuanui garden around their beautiful house the time of the 'Release of the Tui' and it is beautiful. I do believe the rest of the places up there are the same. They are sure making good use of their properties.

Author (centre) with Hana Whaanga (left) and Josie Ormond (right), at the Maori Film Festival in Nuhaka, 2011.

Personal Footnote

Two-thirds of the way through writing this book I suffered a heart attack. I was hospitalised for four weeks, and then again for a couple of days to have my pace-maker inserted. This heart problem had been tormenting my very existence for many years. In fact according to some Doctors, I may have been born with this enlarged heart. During my time of hospitalisation and throughout my convalescence, there were times when I did a lot of soul-searching.

People were so kind that I was overwhelmed with the cards, gifts, flowers and visits from loved ones, and the thoughts and prayers from so many of you. All the daily text messages received by my daughter from you all [you know who you are] were a great comfort. One of my sisters flew from Christchurch to Wellington to visit me for one hour from her earthquake stricken City; that is love – thank you, Sis. Family and friends who prayed for me never 'let-up'. I want to take this opportunity through this page of this booklet to thank you and to emphasise the power of prayer and positive thoughts.

Thanks to my two daughters, especially Jan who never left my side, and Donna and her youngest girl who made a dash down to Wellington Hospital to support Jan during my critically ill period, and again driving me back to Wellington for my first check-up. Also cousin Garry, Aunty Eileen and Uncle Ath for all the visits to the Napier *and* Wellington Hospitals. And my brother Frank for his daily visits.

Thanks to my son Paul and his partner for their *aroha* and concern, and last but not least — my son-in-law Rihi for his *aroha* as well, and for taking great care of the *whanau* for the four weeks Jan was away from them.

Since then, I have made some dramatic changes in my life. Although I am eager to experience my new, calm, organised life, I need to remind myself that there is no rush. The old me would think "I need to rush and complete this book now" — but it is yesterday's belief. My new life has changed to "order happens beautifully from the inside out" by taking one day at a time.

God bless you all who had the patience to wade your way through this non-chronological preamble of my childhood life that wandered with fondness all over the place in time.

"This is ZLDD Owenga (from Nuhaka) calling ZLC Chatham Islands — over and out."

Author's Statement: What it means to me to be Moriori

1994 Statement to the Crown and the Waitangi Tribunal during the hearing of the Moriori Claim

By VALERIE HOANA METE (nee PREECE)

1. My name is Valerie Hoana Mete. I was born at Waitangi, Rehohu in 1938. My mother was Mate Florence Preece, the half sister of Bunty Preece. I was brought up as a child by Bunty's and Eileen's mother and father, Lily and Charlie Preece (Snr). My tipuna is Riwai Te Ropiha and Kiti Karaka who was Moriori and Ngai Tahu.
2. My late husband, Paul Mete, was of Ngati Kahungunu descent. I have three children whose names are Paul, Janetta and Donna. I also have four grandchildren.
3. I left Rekohu in 1952 to attend St Joseph's Maori Girls School in Napier. My guardians in New Zealand were Aunty Stella and Uncle Charlie Cotter.

What it means to me to be Moriori

4. From a young girl I always knew I was Moriori. But no one ever spoke about it as I recall. I was always proud to be Moriori but I didn't know anything about it during my childhood.

5. The most dramatic part of my life was leaving Rekohu and going to St Joseph's Maori Girls School. I remember all of us girls had to stand up and say who we were. All the girls except me were able to mihi about who they were and their tribal whakapapa. Coming from the island and going to live in a Maori community, I felt like a real fish out of water. I knew as far back as the first generation of Moriori but beyond that it was a mystery to me. At that time I lost a lot of confidence in myself. My self esteem was at an all time low because of not knowing very much about who I was.

6. Sometimes when I would tell people I was Moriori I remember that some of them would tell me that there were no such people. It was really difficult and embarrassing when these people were much older and supposedly wiser than I was. I didn't have a base to rely on so I couldn't argue back and I didn't want to argue with them. I just said nothing. But inside it really used to eat away at me.

7. I want to make sure that my children know who they are and know about their Moriori as well as their Kahungunu and Ngai Tahu heritage.

8. When I think back now I realise it wasn't my fault. We were never taught about our culture. The schools didn't teach us about our heritage and what was taught about Moriori was mostly rubbish and myth making. Our own people never spoke about it much either.

9. Aunty Stella used to tell me bits and pieces about what her mother Ngaria told her. I also looked after Ngaria for a while when she was ill and I remember that she showed me a lot of things. I used to go there after school and visit Ngaria. She would get me to collect paua and watercress from certain places. She told me how and what to do. She laid down the kawa to me about these things.

10. I returned to Rekohu in 1968 with me husband and family and stayed until 1971. I loved to go for walks along the beaches through the mist. I sometimes got a real urge to go walking at night along the beach as if my ancestors were beckoning to me. At such times it is as though I can feel my ancestors walking with me. I know that it may sound strange but to me the mist is like the hot breath of my tipuna. It is a comforting feeling having them around me and I get this overwhelming sense of well being.

11. I remember one time after Aunty Myrtle's funeral (Myrtle was Bunty's first wife), I went for a walk in the mist at night. People thought I was mad going out that late at night but I felt that strong urge again. As I was walking along the road at Owenga I could sense my tipuna were with me. At the end of the road near "The Brook", a group of weka came out of the bush and started squawking at me. It was as if they were talking to me. It was as if they were trying to tell me something. I felt as if they were greeting me and welcoming me. I felt as if they said to me it was time to go back. I said "I'm just out for a walk" and told them not to worry. I know that this might sound odd but our ancestors were very spiritual people. To me these things are very real. I believe our Moriori tipuna are watching over us. I know they are.

Moriori revival

12. Although I now live in New Zealand I have never forgotten where I came from. I have just never known up until the last thirty years who I am. To me the continued revival of Moriori culture, history and traditions is vitally important. It is important for a whole number of reasons but for me they are very personal reasons. I know what it was like as a teenager in a situation with one's peers and to feel

embarrassed by the lack of knowledge about one's tribal self. I don't want my children to go through what I went through. I want them to know their waka, their maunga, their whenua and their hokopapa. These are things which other tribes in New Zealand take for granted. These are things which are jealously guarded and passed on to future generations. We as Moriori must be given that same opportunity and the same rights. We have been denied these things for too long.

That is all.

Signed by Valerie Hoana Mete

In Appreciation

An Author can write and re-write, read and re-read the manuscript over and over, and then again and again, and it seems to be fine. Every word seems to conform. At this stage one needs to pass the manuscript onto someone else, which I did. My friend Hana Whaanga read and further edited it, and I want to thank you Hana for reading every word with diligence and thoroughness.

Then I needed an Editor/Publisher. Nancy Kahalewai of "Island Moonlight Publishing" was recommended. From the moment I found her, it was "all go". There was a lot of telecommunication, and Nancy travelled from Gisborne for several months during weekends breaking into her busy work schedule from lecturing at EIT Tairawhiti, as well as working on other publishing projects.

Having no idea just how much was involved in publishing, I soon found out. I felt obligated and excited. We have had lots of to-ing and fro-ing while Nancy put the story into a more chronological order so she could chapter it. Then the Glossary needed to be done, plus scanning the photos and many other tasks. So at this juncture a big thank you goes out to you, Nancy, for all of that, as well as your calm and considerate manner at all times.

The next very important factor was accessing financial assistance to get this book produced, published and marketed. I contacted my Ngai Tahu Iwi who advised me to go to our local Tairawhiti TPK [Te Puni Kokiri] in Gisborne. Within a short time the office of TPK sourced a funding avenue that helps fund Maori writers. Thanks a million to "The Maori Purposes Funding Board" and the Manager and Staff at Gisborne TPK. I am indeed grateful to you all, as this would not have happened otherwise.

I want to also thank the many friends and family members who offered me photos and support, and my own Nuhaka whanau who kept the interest up and kept urging me on, especially the Nuhaka Friendship Club.

Arohanui ki a koutou.

For more about the Chatham Islands, visit:
www.discoverthechathamislands.co.nz

Family Photos

Uncle Bunty with his family.

Uncle Charlie, Uncle Bunty and Reverend Riwai.

Myrtle and Bunty cooking crayfish, 1984.

(Left to right): Val, Uncle Charlie, Aunty Cissie, and husband Paul.

Family Photos 171

Charlie, Reverend Riwai, Bunty and Eileen.

Aunty Myrtle, Uncle Bunty, Uncle Charlie and Aunty Cissie enjoying some island cuisine, 1984.

Catholic priest, Eileen and Athol on way home, Port Waikato.

Val with brothers Alan and Frank.

Family Photos 173

Mother, Father behind in Christchurch with Eileen, Riwai and Herbert.

Friends and relatives at church. Val's birthmother Mate is in back row, far left.

(Left to right): Bunty, Elaine, Val, Eileen, Wayne, Gary and Stella at Moriori hearing in Wellington, about 1996.

Eileen and Val with cousins James and Gregory Preece, 2004.

Family Photos 175

My aunties looking sporty in their uniforms, circa 1947.

Uncle Charlie looking very handsome in his suit.

Recipes

Kaeo or Sea-Tulips

Harvesting: Found in Owenga only on Cloughs Beach, it washed up in kelp after a certain wind. This wind blew in off the sea. Unfortunately, this didn't happen very often. In their oval kelp case that is attached to a long string of kelp, it reminds me of a long poi.

Preparation: Split case open with knife — slip food out with thumb, it looks something like a mussel. You can eat them raw or marinated in water, sugar and vinegar. You can batter them or cut them into pieces and make fritters.

Kaeo have a taste of their own and one does need to acquire this taste. I wouldn't expect anyone who hasn't eaten them as a child to savour them like we do. They are my favourite.

Kotoretore Soup

Aunty Ellen Goomes passed this recipe onto me when she was cooking at Feron's Fish Factory in Owenga.
Kotoretore are commonly known as sun-sets to us, but they are sea anemone in the marine book, and *kotoretore* to the Maori. They are unique because they do not have a shell and

the whole morsel is edible. Interestingly, they often blocked the salt water pipes that fed the Factory, and became a continuous nuisance to the workers.

Gathering: These are mainly found in the rock pools where the sand is gritty. My favourite place is down the cattle-yards on Owenga Station, in the pools closest to the beach. When you get your first glimpse of them they are in their full glory, opened up in the pool looking like a big sunset, or like the flower after which they are named, the sea anemone.

You need to put your hand very quickly into the pool, dig down, and give a twist using your hand like a gardening trowel. They are very very sensitive, and as soon as they feel vibrations or the slightest touch on the surface of the water, they quickly close up and disappear under the sand. Where there is one, there will be a bed of them. I hope I haven't put you off harvesting them. This may sound like an ordeal but believe me, it's not so hard.

Preparation: Open up the sun-set and scrape off the grit, cut them into bite-sized pieces and put into a saucepan with some water. Add onions, carrots and peas (optional), salt and pepper. Boil for about one minute, then simmer until carrots are cooked. You can thicken with a little corn flour or ordinary flour mixed with water, or leave as is and serve as a soup if you wish.

Presentation: Serve with crusty bread or toast.

Baked Kotoretore

After cleaning off any grit, put into a shallow dish [I use an enamel plate], cover with nobs of butter, pepper and salt and bake in oven until tender. Keep checking by poking with a fork until tender, and like all seafood, they don't take long to cook. Overcooking will toughen them. To me they are the next best thing next to a *paua*.

Presentation: Serve like you would any other seafood – with a side salad of mesculin, tomato wedges, thin red onion rings and a thin slice of lemon twisted.

Another option: Serve with a sweet and sour sauce.

Ngakihi or Limpids

This shellfood has a conical shell and clings to the rocks with its muscular foot. The biggest limpids worth eating were found on the flat rocks at the Manukau Point.

<u>Harvesting</u>: Lift limpid off rocks with a long blade knife. Push food out with thumb.

You will find that the roe is like a *kina* tongue, and it actually does taste like a *kina*, which were one of our favourites. As kids we would kick them loose off the rocks.

Take food out, take teeth out plus the thin cotton-like thread that runs around the inside of the flesh. You can now eat them as is, or marinate in a brine of water, sugar and vinegar like one would do *paua*. Some older people liked them after they had soaked overnight in water. We ate them with bread and butter.

I am sorry now for not concentrating more when Nan was telling me – the *korero* (story) of the Ngakihi. All I remember is that the shell resembles a Moriori *waka* (canoe; boat) - the teeth looked like fishhooks, and the thread around the circumference of the inside of the shell was like the fishing line.

Paieke / Parengo / Karengo or Sea Lettuce

Harvesting: This is harvested during the winter months after it has turned brown. Pull or cut it off the rocks. Washing is optional, as the sea has been swishing over it during the high tide.

We put it in a big oven dish with a little water and a heap of butter, and baked it slowly for about half a day, or more or less until it was soft and ready for consumption. Nowadays we cook it in a slow-cooker or crockpot on low heat. Simmer, add more water only if necessary. Too much water could make it tasteless.

Another option: Some people like to add a bit of bacon to the pot.

Glossary
Maori terms used in this book

Ake ake — native tree
Awhi — care for
Haangi — food cooded in an earth oven
Harakeke — flax
Inanga — overgrown whitebait
Kaanga Kopiro — fermented corn
Kaeo — sea tulip
Kai — food
Kaimoana — seafood
Karaka — native tree with berries
Karakia — prayer
Kawa — underlying rules and protocol
Kawakawa — native medicinal pepper plant
Kete — woven flax kit or basket
Kina — sea urchin
Koha — gift
Kopakopa — plantain
Kopi — edible berry from native Karaka tree
Korari — flax flower
Korau — wild turnip
Koromiko — native medicinal plant (hebe)

Korero — story
Kotero — fermented potatoes
Kotoretore — sea anemones
Kotutu — boil-up
Kuku — mussel
Mahi — work
Mai na ano — earlier times, from long ago
Manuka — medicinal native shrub
Maori — indigenous people of Aotearoa, New Zealand
Marae — tribal meeting house
Miti tahu — meat preserved in fat
Moana — ocean, sea
Mokopuna — grandchildren
Moriori — indigenous people of Rekohu, the Chatham Islands

Pakeke — potato fritters
Paua — abalone
Paieke — sea lettuce
Pakeke — potatoe fritters
Pikau bags — split sacks
Pipi — shell fish, aka tuatua
Pono — absolute truth
Poroporo — edible night shade
Puha — edible milk thistle
Raupa — cracked skin
Rekohu — Moriori name for Chatham Islands
Rongoa — medicine
Taere — small mussel
Taewa — potato

Tahu — preserving in its own fat
Taiko — native bird
Tamariki — children
Tangaroa — God of the Sea
Tawhirimatea — wind
Tikanga — customs and procedures
Titi — mutton bird
Tipuna — elders
Turangawaewae — spiritual home
Urupa — cemetary
Wahi tapu — sacred place
Waka — boat; canoe
Weka — edible bird, woodhen
Whakapapa — family; lineage
Whaka whanaungatanga — caring for family;
    kindness and hospitality

Whanau — family
Whanau marae — meeting house for the extended family
Whare — house
Wharekauri — Maori name for the Chathams
Whenua — land

www.ingramcontent.com/pod-product-compliance
Lightning Source LLC
Chambersburg PA
CBHW061305110426
42742CB00012BA/2059